Parts and Memory Therapy

The Clinical Guide

Also by Jay Noricks

As Linguist and Anthropologist

A Tuvalu Dictionary, Two Volumes: Tuvalu-English; English-Tuvalu.

As Psychologist/Psychotherapist

Parts Psychology

For Women Only, Book 1

Healing Amelia

Article: Women's Issues

How Parts and Memory Therapy with Memory Reconsolidation Bring Remission to Premenstrual Dysphoric Disorder (PMDD). The Science of Psychotherapy February, 2020: 24-41.

PARTS AND MEMORY THERAPY

THE CLINICAL GUIDE

JAY NORICKS PHD

NEW UNIVERSITY PRESS LLC
WWW.NEWUNIVERSITYPRESS.COM
LOS ANGELES • LAS VEGAS

Copyright © 2022 by Jay Noricks
Cover Copyright © 2022 by Siena Holland

Printed in the United States of America

All rights reserved.
Except for brief quotes in reviews and scientific citations, no part of this book may be reproduced, translated, stored in a retrieval system, or transmitted in any form or by any means, electric, mechanical, photocopying, microfilming, recording, or otherwise, without written permission of the author or the publisher.

For permissions, write to:

Editor
New University Press LLC
9402 W. Lake Mead Blvd
Las Vegas NV 89134
Or:
Dina@partsandmemorytherapy.com

ISBN 978-0-9969291-1-0

LCCN: 2021949502

Acknowledgements

Full credit for giving me the time and support to write this book belongs to Dina Noricks, my wife, partner and colleague in psychotherapy. When the need to write overtook me, and I saw fewer patients for a while, Dina managed both our household and our work demands. She's had my back, always.

I'm also grateful to all of my patients over the last 25 years for their courage to buy into a new and challenging type of therapy and for their gift of sharing their inner worlds, their inscapes, with me. Without the 44,000 hours of "Parts work" they shared with me, there would be no Parts and Memory Therapy (P&MT).

My trainers and I have continued to expand our outreach to therapists in other cities, states, and overseas. Thanks to this first group of trainers: Dina Noricks, Patrick Tobey, and Preston Walker. Now these trainers are helping us train new ambassadors/trainers to do their own workshops as we expand into new territories. This group of trainers-in-training include Anthony Lee, Lauren McGauley, Theresa Noonan, Samantha Rich, Deissy Rosenbaum, Dominique Wilson, and Kimberly Wood.

Many of those who attend our workshop repeat it at a later date and some sign up for and complete the advanced training to qualify for "Certified" status. This growing team of practitioners, from a variety of subdisciplines, have done the work to become experts (Certified) in doing Parts and Memory Therapy. Currently, they include Nicole Cauchois (CPC), Denise Hooks (CPC), Kelley Johnson (LCSW), Kristin Kakiuchi (MFT), Natalie Kaufman (MFT), Sarah Marmon (CPC), Theresa Noonan (MFT), Jessica Mix-Tesmer (MFT), Marta Pagan-Trevino (CPC), Jossie Schauerhamer (MFT), Miranda Schreiber (CPC), and Ashanti Shakir (MFT).

Finally, I thank my editors: Stevie Miller who corrected my language and grammar in early drafts, and Zetta and Jim Brown, who did the final proofreading and formatting, respectively.

Rica Bonaccorsi provided invaluable last-minute guidance in the insertion of tables I had poorly organized. My daughter Darcy Noricks was always there to fix my problems with Word and to offer feedback as the book developed. My daughter Siena Holland illustrated the front cover of the book and formatted the complete cover. My son Jacob Noricks guided me with the intense concentration required for the Index. Three of my colleagues, Hugh Marr, Thomas Hill, and Esly Carvalho, took time away from their own busy schedules to read my manuscript. I am grateful for their insightful comments and suggestions for emphasis and clarification.

Preface

Parts and Memory Therapy: The Clinical Guide is the culmination of more than 20 years of exploration and practice of psychotherapy. This clinical guide results from my belated recognition that the short theoretical overviews of the P&MT model I presented for each of my three previous psychotherapy books were not sufficient for other therapists to teach themselves all of the ins and outs of the model. This guide aims to be that standalone resource for therapists wishing to learn or adapt the model to their own ways of thinking and doing psychotherapy.

I originally called P&MT "Parts Psychology." In my last two books, however, I changed the name of the approach because Parts are only half of the most significant components. The other half involves the emphasis on memories as the source of continuing mental health issues and the primary means of bringing them to remission. Both titles may be used interchangeably, but I now favor the title that includes "memory."

I first learned about Parts of the self in the late 1990s when I stumbled upon a published interview of Richard C. Schwartz answering questions about how narrative therapy and his *Internal Family Systems* (1995) were alike or different. Soon after that I discovered John and Helen Watkins's *Ego States* (1997) and Roberto Assagioli's *Psychosynthesis* (1965), specifically the work of Gretchen Sliker (1992). In rapid order, I discovered the later work of Morton Prince (1925), who first presented the idea that all people have "sides," i.e., "Parts" in the modern sense of multiplicity, and Francine Shapiro (2001), who acknowledged that ego states (Parts) were sometimes activated by her EMDR processing protocol.

Finally, the *International Society for the Study of Trauma and Dissociation (ISSTD)* provided 12 years of heated discussion and argument about whether having Parts of the self is normal or abnormal, and whether alters (Parts) should be integrated into a singular mind through fusing all Parts of the self into a single entity, leaving behind no boundaries that once set off different Parts from each other.

From this early mix came Parts and Memory Therapy. It was through the ISSTD-sponsored discussion groups that I met the late Louis Tinnin, MD, who twice invited me to present Keynote Addresses (2005, 2007) to his and Linda Gantt's *Treating Trauma and Dissociation* Annual Meetings (2005, 2007), sponsored jointly by their Institute and the West Virginia University School of Medicine. Lou's enthusiasm for my work encouraged me to write about my view of Parts of the self, and I eventually did so in *Parts Psychology* (Noricks, 2011).

The single most powerful impact upon my broader thinking was Shapiro's (2001) assertion that virtually all mental health disorders derive from trauma or trauma-like experiences, especially during childhood. While I leaned theoretically toward John and Helen Watkins's ego state work, I was strongly influenced by Richard C. Schwartz, as seen in my heavy use of "unburdening" in my first therapy book (2011). At that time, although I used the term "neutralize" with my own patients, I was hesitant to introduce into the early development of the P&MT model a new term that might appear to be splitting hairs. But I should have done so because the concepts of "unburdening" and "neutralizing" mean quite different things.

Neutralizing is strictly and ultimately about memories. Even when they appear not to be so, as when a patient says her problems are about beliefs that conflict with family, or when another patient says he cannot connect certain unpleasant body feelings or emotions to any of his memories, the link is still there. It's impossible for it to be otherwise. Everything we feel, think, or believe ultimately derives from our life experiences as they are encoded in memories. The only exception I can think of as possibly deriving from another source would be the unlikely possibility that certain of our thoughts, feelings or beliefs could be scientifically proven to derive from genetically-driven sources.

List of Tables

Table 1 The Parts and Memory Therapy Protocol..............13
Table 2 The Parts and Memory Therapy Protocol..........23
Table 3 Protocol for the Step Back Technique................44
Table 4 Protocol for the Twinning Intervention...............46
Table 5 The Parts and Memory Therapy Protocol..........67
Table 6 The Parts and Memory Therapy Protocol..........75
Table 7 Guide to Therapist's Direct Unmasking of Introjects..107
Table 8 The Parts and Memory Therapy Protocol..........137
Table 9 Parts and Memory Therapy Training Protocol...139
Table 10 The Shortcut Protocol..144
Table 11 The Hotspot Trauma Protocol...........................147
Table 12 Letting Go of Love Protocol...............................149
Table 13 Protocol for Trichotillomania and Excoriation..151
Table 14 Protocol for Treatment of Addictions................153
Table 15 Protocol for Treatment of IBS, Fibromyalgia...155
Table 16 Premenstrual Dysphoric Disorder Symptoms..156
Table 17 PMS/PMDD 22 Symptom Ratings....................158
Table 18 Protocol for Treatment of PMS/PMDD..........159
Table 19 Utilizing a Parental Surrogate in Treatment of a Mute Child..162

Contents

Acknowledgements..v

Preface...vii

List of Tables..x

Chapter 1 Introduction to Parts and Memory Therapy......1

Chapter 2 Define the Problem...13

Chapter 3 Find the Part that carries the problem...........23

Chapter 4 Parts Dynamics..43

Chapter 5 Elicit the Memories That Are the
    Foundation for theProblem...........................67

Chapter 6 Neutralize the Problem Memories 75

Chapter 7 Parts and Memory Therapy Protocols..........137

References..163

Glossary..167

Index...171

Chapter 1

Introduction to Parts and Memory Therapy

This book provides a clinical guide for psychotherapists and counselors in the use of Parts and Memory Therapy (P&MT) to treat emotional or psychological problems. Additionally, the book aims to present a clear and compelling narrative for lay persons who wish to know about the latest cutting-edge developments in psychotherapy. For both audiences, this chapter provides a brief introduction to the basic P&MT concepts and tools utilized throughout the book. They are the foundation for the treatment protocols that follow in later chapters.

What Are Parts?

A "Part" with a capital "P" is the term I use to reference what other scholars call parts, ego states, sides, subpersonalities, voices, self-states, etc. I will sometimes use the word "subpersonality" or "ego state" in place of "Part" to avoid monotony and also to make specific grammatical issues easier to negotiate. These terms refer to natural subdivisions in what we usually call our personality or our self. The bottom line is that the self or personality is not unitary; it's made up of many Parts.

There are two primary types of Parts regularly addressed in the P&MT paradigm: *Freestanding (FS) Parts* and *Stuck-in-the-Memory (SIM) Parts*. These labels represent structural units in the organization of mind and memory. They arose naturally, empirically, from the study of the inscape, the largely nonconscious world of Parts of the self—instead of labels imposed from without that draw upon *a priori* assumptions from other theories (e.g., Freudian, Jungian, or Family Systems concepts). There are other Parts, where labels based upon function, such as angry Part or professional Part, apply, but FS and SIM Parts represent a deeper structure within the nonconscious mind. FS Parts are what most scholars are talking about when they use terms like ego state, subpersonality, voice, etc. They rarely, if ever, talk about SIM Parts. But for Parts and Memory Therapy, the distinction is crucial.

Freestanding Parts

FS Parts are the aspects of self we refer to when we say, "A Part of me wants to break up with him/her, but another Part can't imagine life without him/her." This format of "a Part...this and a Part...that" is one we apply to countless conflicts either individually or relationally throughout our lives. Parts are everywhere. They are the sources of our feelings of sadness, anger, fear, and other mood states when they blend with the self.

In the therapy room, they are the entities we seek out and then guide in healing problematic memories, which in turn heal the disturbing emotional states our patients bear. They are also the entities that serve as storage units of our memories. When we look for the source of our patients' dysfunctions, we consult with FS Parts to find the memories that cause the dysfunctions.

An FS Part has been emancipated from any single memory to host its own unique set of themed memories. It isn't merely a self-representation of a single high-energy moment, such as when your parent died or when you first viewed your first-born child. An FS Part has a set of memories that has shaped its personality and function. It is co-conscious with the self or is capable of being so.

The FS Part generally contains within its set of memories a total that ranges from a small number up to a set of memories that charts the lifespan of the patient. When the patient talks about memories, she draws upon the FS Parts' memory sets that blend with her consciousness at that time. She has no memories that are uniquely her own, but she has access to all the memories of her FS Parts, except for a few likely-painful memories that are intentionally kept from her by well-meaning managers.

When visualized, these Parts might appear to be younger or differently-dressed versions of the patient. The Part might also draw upon more symbolic imagery, such as an angry Part appearing as a devil, a monster, or a ball of fire. But regardless of how an FS Part presents itself, the image represents a Part of the person that can think, communicate, and make decisions.

The following example illustrates the limit of coconsciousness in an FS Part. It's instructive to be aware of the variation at the margins of the types of Parts we've located.

For example, in working with a bulimic, 22-year-old female patient, I located a Part that acquired a disturbing memory at age 11 when a family member made a negative comment about her weight. Following the P&MT protocol, we neutralized the negative energy connected to the memory. But we then discovered that the 11-year-old, apparently a SIM Part, had memories of other rude remarks about the patient's body as far back as two years. Further, although what at first appeared to be a SIM Part had no general knowledge about events in my patient's life since the age of 11 (it believed my patient was still 11), it was aware of exactly what she had eaten that week and could name each item in each meal. It acknowledged that it was behind the urge to purge, but it was not the Part that drove the binging. Nor did it remember the actual events of purging. It was coconscious with the patient for the brief time it took to finish each meal.

The 11-year-old SIM Part was not a SIM Part after all, but instead, a minimal sort of FS Part with a situationally specific ability to share consciousness with the patient at mealtimes. It also experienced something close to consciousness when it somehow influenced my patient to purge through vomiting or long-distance running. My patient identified this Part as a significant source of her urge to purge even though it did not have current-time purging memories. It remained at 11 years old.

The Conscious Self

To avoid confusion with the language of other scholars who attempt to define "the self," I have chosen a new term, the "Conscious Self," to stand for what self implies in Parts and Memory Therapy. Unless the context suggests otherwise, self is synonymous with Conscious Self. I also use the term loosely to refer to the patient with whom we communicate as we do psychotherapy.

It's difficult to pin down exactly which entity deserves the label of "self." It's fuzzy. Even FS Parts sometimes disagree about who is the self. The Parts who regularly blend to represent the Conscious Self are in relatively close agreement, but in the nonconscious inscape, some Parts may be unaware of the passage of time and may believe that a vulnerable Part they are protecting—perhaps a sensitive 5-year-old or an anxious 11-year-old preadolescent—is the self.

For this guide (and subject to change if evidence shows otherwise), I think of the self as consisting of a core of conscious awareness combined with a manager who has a strong sense of being the "I" or "me" of the person (but is buffeted this way and that by FS Parts that are sometimes in agreement and sometimes in conflict). The FS Parts, which regularly blend with the Conscious Self, provide a sense of character or personality that others view as the essence of who we are. As a label, "Conscious Self" has the advantage of implying that other elements, perhaps nonconscious ones, may also be involved in the whole person's makeup.

The Conscious Self is then a blended group of Parts that project the familiar personality we show to others. But the members of the group that constitute the Conscious Self vary, depending upon the context. It includes a sad Part when a joyless situation unfolds, an angry Part when an injustice is present, or a fearful Part when there is danger, etc. And sometimes, there are Parts present that blend with the Conscious Self but are not paying attention, such as an FS child Part that ignores the activities of other Parts when the Conscious Self engages in everyday work activity that has nothing of interest to the child Part.

Stuck-in-the-Memory Parts

A SIM (Stuck-in-the-Memory) Part represents a person as he was at the time of the traumatic or other high-energy memory of our focus. In the memory of high school graduation, a patient's view of himself (from outside himself), walking across the stage for his diploma and handshake would be a SIM Part. In another memory, if he can see himself as a little boy in the memory of his first physical beating by his mother, he would be viewing a SIM Part. He has as many SIM Parts as he has autobiographical memories. He could have hundreds of such Parts, the total number depending upon how many high-energy moments of his life he can identify.

Generally, each SIM Part has only the one memory—the one in which we uncovered it. However, when there are similar high-energy events nearby in time or space the same SIM Part may also be embedded in the other memories, too. This means that when we finish neutralizing the first emotional memory we are given, we need to check for other memories of the SIM Part before moving on.

Fuzzy Types of Parts

I've sometimes used the label "stuck-in-time Part" for Stuck-in-the-Memory Part in workshops and other discussions. I no longer do so because I've found it creates more confusion than clarity. By definition, Stuck-in-the-Memory Parts would also be stuck-in-time Parts, since memories always capture moments in past time. But sometimes, Parts that are stuck in time more closely resemble FS Parts than the SIM Parts that appear in single memories.

For example, in seeking the source of a particular present-time emotion or belief, we might find a 10-year-old apparent SIM Part that is unaware of current events in a patient's adult life. And it may have several earlier memories, perhaps from as early as age three or four, over which it considers itself the manager, which suggests it is an FS Part. It can be triggered by current events that share the themes that organize its own set of memories, and we generally need to have permission to work with any of its earlier memories. In these ways, it's like an FS Part, but lacks coconsciousness with the Conscious Self.

For these reasons, plus the fact that it can quickly learn to connect with and cooperate with the Conscious Self, I now label this sort of stuck-in-time art as a Freestanding (FS) Part. Such a Part was probably once an FS Part with everyday access to conscious experience. But it was left behind as the person grew up and moved on with Parts older and better adapted to adulthood's changing conditions. I will explain below how this works.

Memory Reconsolidation

Later chapters describe many other variations in how Parts present themselves. But before we go deeper into how Parts and Memory Therapy work, I want to refer to the scientific literature that supports our use of visualizations to permanently neutralize the emotional memories that lead to psychological dysfunction.

Our interventions take advantage of *memory reconsolidation*, a recently discovered natural neurological process in memory formation and reformation. As utilized in the P&MT model, it permits us to neutralize the disturbing implicit emotional memories (such as fear, grief, anger, shock, etc.) that give emotional color to their explicit traumatic or trauma-like, factual life narratives.

We do this by coaching our patients to visualize the permanent disappearance or destruction of the emotions or body sensations created when the targeted memories were formed. Previously, such emotional memories were thought to be indelible, unchangeable. (See Duvarci and

Nader, 2004; Pedreira et al., 2002; Pedreira and Maldonado, 2003; Walker et al., 2003 [cited in Ecker, 2018]).

Emotional Memories.
As described below, emotional memories are the sources of most adult psychological dysfunction. Recently, the work on memory reconsolidation by neuroscientists was imported into psychotherapy by Bruce Ecker and colleagues (Ecker et al., 2012; Ecker, 2015; Ecker, 2018). Although some psychotherapists were already doing work that could be characterized as driven by memory reconsolidation (e.g., H. Watkins, 1980; Schwartz, 1995; Noricks, 2011), it wasn't until Ecker and his colleagues translated the neuroscientific work into psychotherapy that we acquired a neuroscientific explanation of why our interventions were working.

Destabilize, Neutralize, Reconsolidate.
As understood in Parts and Memory Therapy, memory reconsolidation is a process such that, during recollection of a targeted memory, and with the aid of the Stuck-in-the-Memory Part that originally experienced the remembered event, the emotional memories become destabilized and subject to editing. In our approach the essential element in destabilization of the targeted memory is the mismatch between what the Stuck-in-the-Memory Part would expect, given the context of its life at the time the memory was created, and what the therapist brings to its reactivation: understanding, empathy, and helpful concern. This, along with the intervention that visualizes the disappearance of the original negative emotions, neutralizes (erases) the

original negative emotions and replaces them with emotional neutrality (See Ecker, 2018 for an extended, more technical explanation of the role of a mismatch.)

The editing out, or erasing, of the original emotions and body sensations through visualizing their disappearance ultimately leads to the reconsolidation of the targeted memory into the current, therapeutic reality, one in which the targeted memory lacks any emotional impact at all. The patient is neutral for the original memory, although he will remember that it was once painful. The original memory can no longer be triggered or emotionally experienced as traumatic or troubling. Emotionally, the memories are neither negative nor positive. Within a few hours following the intervention, memory reconsolidation is complete and the changes are permanent.

Silent Abreaction, Unburdening, Neutralizing.
Memory reconsolidation seems to have been the active element in the intervention Helen Watkins called the "silent abreaction" (H. Watkins, 1980; Watkins & Watkins, 1997). She utilized hypnosis to activate a patient's angry "ego state" and then reduced that anger through the symbolic visualization of exhausting the ego state's anger through its battering of a physical obstacle on an imagined walk in the mountains.

Richard C. Schwartz later developed his Internal Family Systems therapy (Schwartz, 1995) in which he applied his concept of "unburdening" to bringing permanent relief to subpersonalities that carry burdens of emotional pain from their accumulated life experiences.

In my previous books (Noricks, 2011, 2014, 2018), I introduced the term "neutralize" for the process by which we coach a patient to visualize the symbolic release of the disturbing emotional energy still bound to the autobiographical memories identified as sources of current dysfunction. Each of the above three models appears to depend upon memory reconsolidation to bring about permanent change in emotional memories.

Mismatch Plus Positive Visualization.
To summarize: In Parts and Memory Therapy, the necessary mismatches are the visualizations we use to overwrite the memory circuits' existing neural pathways with neutrality in place of the expectation of continued pain. Rather than continued pain, the patient finds her pain, sadness, or shame visualized as blown away, washed away, or incinerated. We might even encourage the patient to coach the SIM Part to simply throw the negative emotions into the trash, if that intervention served the patient as sufficiently powerful. The memory circuit's destabilized condition permits us to make these neutralizing changes to emotional memories. However, within a few hours of our interventions, the targeted memory circuits reconsolidate, synapses lock again, and the changes become permanent.

Chapter 2

Define the Problem

In formulating a description of the problem, you must help your patient state the problem simply. Identifying the problem is the direct route to discovering the Part that carries the problem for your patient. In work with dissociative identity disorder, where a Part has already presented itself, this step is easily accomplished simply by interviewing the Part when it takes executive control of your patient.

Table 1. The Parts and Memory Therapy Protocol

The basic protocol for all P&MT work contains just four steps. They are easily stated, but much more complex when put into action.

1. ***DEFINE THE PROBLEM.***
2. Find the Part that carries the problem.
3. Elicit the memories that are the foundation for the problem.
4. Neutralize the problem memories.

Diagnosis vs. Symptoms.
Diagnosis is essential for communicating with other professionals and for qualifying our patients for insurance coverage and billing. But diagnosis is not the focus of identifying the problems we treat. We are interested in a patient's symptoms and, especially, her description of her problematic or conflictual personal beliefs and felt emotions.

Vague Problems.
Vague or broadly stated problems are more difficult to deal with than more specific ones. For example, a problem stated as "low self-esteem" could be difficult to link to any given Part. There might be several Parts who could say they have low self-esteem. The difficulty lies in the absence of a hook you can use to find the Part. The hook would be an emotion, a body sensation, or a firmly-held belief or attitude. I might ask a patient with a problem of low self-esteem how she knows she has low self-esteem or what does she feel that tells her she has low self-esteem. For example, she might say, "When I'm around important people, I clam up and become shy." That statement would then allow you to ask her, "What does it feel like when you clam up and become shy?" If she says, "My shoulders get tense," or "My stomach is in a knot," excellent! You can work with that. You can ask her to visualize the Part of her who feels tense or knotted. The body sensation will guide you to the Part.

Body Sensations.
Suppose a patient says that he cannot stand being around his in-laws, which causes a problem with his wife. He cannot identify a body sensation that accompanies his feelings toward his in-laws, but he knows he doesn't like them. He may experience his dislike as residing in his head rather than his body. You could ask him to focus on that dislike—maybe think of some things that temporarily increase his dislike—and then request that he visualize the Part of himself that feels this dislike.

Initially, we will define the problem in terms of the symptoms described by the patient. For example, the patient may say she is depressed. Further probing may give us the information that what she means by depressed is that she is sad, tired, and bored, or has a diminished interest in what she usually likes to do. We can utilize the body sensations of these symptoms to guide us on the Parts that experience them and bring them to the awareness of the Conscious Self. The symptoms guide us to the royal road to the underlying problem memories. These memories are generally disturbing in some way, although sometimes the problems can rest on a foundation of original positive experiences, such as when romantic love outlasts a permanent breakup, or with pornographic arousal connected to inappropriate relationships.

Problem Beliefs.
Problematic attitudes or beliefs work in the same way. A man who views the world through a paranoid lens likely feels emotions or body sensations that accompany his be-

liefs. His fear might present itself as distrust or anger toward particular others. I would want to help him discover and articulate how he experiences distrust as an emotion or sensation. Stating the problem as an emotional experience rather than a cognition (a thought or piece of knowledge) is a better strategy. It's easier to bridge from an emotion to a Part than from a cognition to a Part. Still, it's sometimes possible for a patient to focus upon a belief and, in the absence of experienced emotion or body sensation, to ask that belief to show itself through an image of a Part.

Dissociated Memories.

Patients may delay defining the problem when beginning therapy and say something like, "My childhood was perfect. I had the best parents, great support, friends, and school, no problems at all." This explanation begs the question of why the person is seeking therapy in the first place. If he has come for couples therapy only because his wife demands it, that doesn't bode well for the relationship. No one escapes childhood and growing up without emotional wounds.

The myth of a perfect childhood and perfect growing up results from an efficient system of normal dissociation that moves the pains of growing up out of awareness and into a kind of apparent limbo. But painful memories don't go away just because they're out of your awareness. They continue to percolate unconsciously and may silently enter your consciousness in emotional ways, such as untethered body tension or snappy emotional responses to your spouse. Finding the emotional memories linked to these experiences is essential to successful treatment with Parts and Memory Therapy.

Normal Dissociation.
Dissociation is a normal process in all humans. It permits us to continue living our lives without being overcome by experiences that would keep us stuck indefinitely in the pain of a disturbing event. It's also possible (to the detriment of normal functioning) to get stuck in the joyful energy of a positive one-off experience. Dissociation is frequently described as an abnormal process, especially in the context of discussions of dissociative disorders, such as dissociative identity disorder. However, it's the normal process by which we manage to continue our lives despite setbacks, large and small. For example, if a teacher shames a child when he fails to turn in his homework, that shame could be so great that he might not return to class without help. The continuing shame might be too great for him to engage in everyday activities. He needs the natural process that separates the trauma from everyday life. Then he can return to class.

Dissociation, as noted above, isn't limited to negative emotional experiences. It applies as well to any high-energy experience, including joyful ones such as the birth of a child, winning or doing well in a contest, or graduation from schools or colleges. Normal dissociation is necessary for all of us. Otherwise, even our small hurts or our successes would stay fully present in our consciousness and prevent us from adapting to the next moment's challenge.

Mild Dissociation and Amnesia

Amnesia for traumatic life experiences is a recognized symptom of pathological dissociation. It immediately raises the question of whether the patient might have a dissociative disorder, perhaps even dissociative identity disorder if she displays alternating executive control by alter personalities (i.e., by Parts of self). Unfortunately, many, perhaps most, students of dissociation don't recognize dissociation's role in more normal forgetfulness. Below are four examples of the role of dissociation and amnesia in the lives of dissociatively normal persons. The amnesia became apparent only when I had the opportunity to interview the patients' known Freestanding Parts.

Example 1: Destroying a Meal.
In the first example, my patient—who came to therapy to process her resentments toward a disinterested husband—described her embarrassment at cooking her worst meal ever when her husband invited a new neighborhood friend to dinner. Every item was a disaster: main course, vegetables, and dessert. She could not explain what happened. She prided herself on her cooking skills and could not understand how she produced such an embarrassing meal. At the same time, she was not displeased that their guest would not be coming back. She disliked him and believed that he was of questionable character.

Because I believed that such simple accidents are often the results of influence by internal Parts, I asked if she would be willing to survey the Parts we knew to see if they were aware of what caused the poorly cooked meal. Indeed, we found a Part that admitted sabotaging the meal—because it didn't want a continuing relationship with the neighbor. It acknowledged influencing my patient to over-cook the meat, over-salt the vegetables, and omit the desert's sugar.

Example 2: Misplaced Love Note.
The second example comes from a session with a man who had come to therapy to help him decide whether he wanted to divorce his wife or reclaim a faltering marriage. I'll call him Mark. He was currently having an affair with a coworker. While he didn't share the professed love his coworker declared for him, he enjoyed the experience and occasionally considered whether they might have a future together. Mark's wife was an attractive woman with whom he shared two grown children, both in college, but whose "controlling" personality led him to hold onto years of resentments toward her

During the week following a session in which we began working on neutralizing these resentments, his wife discovered his affair. In our next session, Mark described the puzzling event that caught him out. He awakened on a Sunday morning with his wife demanding an explanation. She had discovered a love note from his girlfriend tucked underneath her keys where she usually left them on the kitchen counter. Mark had no idea how the love note got from his pocket calendar's pages to the spot under his wife's keys on the counter.

He agreed to consult with some of his FS Parts that we had come to know from our previous work. Very quickly, Mark discovered the sabotage by one of the Parts that disliked his wife. This Part admitted that it wanted Mark to divorce his wife. It acknowledged that it had taken the opportunity late on Saturday night, when Mark was tired from a long day of work, and a couple of beers after work, to take brief executive control of Mark's body to slip the love note out of his pocket calendar and under his wife's keys. Its admitted motivation was to reveal the affair in hopes that the wife would divorce Mark. She did.

Example 3: Locked Door.
In the third example, my patient, Joan, was in therapy to discuss a career change. She believed she was getting too old for her sales career and considering going to graduate school to prepare for a different career. She was happy in her marital relationship but noted that she found it difficult to let go of her anger when her husband sometimes spoke to her critically. She described an event in which she had inadvertently locked the door between the garage and the house through which her husband usually passed when he came home from work. She laughed when she recalled the incident, saying maybe she should speed up her transition to a new career before her absentmindedness got her in trouble with her present one.

She agreed to check with the FS Parts we had previously located to see if any might remember accidentally locking out her husband. She learned from two of them—a task manager and an anger manager—that they did indeed remember. And it wasn't an accident. They admitted secretly influencing Joan to "absentmindedly" lock the door. They did so out of spite because they were still upset with him for being critical of her during a conversation the day before.

Example 4: Session No-Show.
In the fourth case, my usually dependable 41-year-old patient, Henry, failed to show up for his session. He called three hours later and apologized. He said that he "totally spaced" the session. In the following session, he agreed to look inside to see if any of his FS Parts had anything to do with his missed appointment.

Henry quickly located the powerful 7-year-old Part we had worked with during the previous three sessions. This Part readily acknowledged the sabotage, saying that it was afraid that we were trying to make it disappear. This child Part had built an alliance with other influential Parts and, with their help, caused Henry to "forget" that he had an appointment with me. They believed that therapy was a threat to them.

Further questioning revealed that Henry had not been following my guidance for neutralizing painful memories. Rather than making the emotional memories neutral while retaining the autobiographical narrative, he had been trying to make the entire autobiographical experiences disappear from memory. These were experiences in which the 7-year-old Part had suffered significant abuse by Henry's parents. Henry, under the influence of a confused 14-year-old Part, tried to delete the painful memories of abuse in their entirety, including the presence of the 7-year-old, rather than retain a neutral record of abusive experiences. Believing that their continued existence was in danger, the 7-year-old's alliance of Parts had caused Henry to forget about coming to our scheduled session. In actuality, it's extremely difficult to make Parts disappear, and certainly far beyond the knowledge or ability of Henry or the 14-year-old Part.

Chapter 3

Find the Part that Carries the Problem

Finding the FS Part that acknowledges being the Part with the problem permits us to begin eliciting the memories we must neutralize if we are to fix the problem. The FS Part is, in effect, the owner (stakeholder) of the set of memories we seek. In the simplest cases, and with a cooperative FS Part, we can quickly neutralize its problem memories from earliest to latest and heal or make a major dent in the issue brought by the patient. More often than not, however, the

---

Table 2. The Parts and Memory Therapy Protocol

The basic protocol for all P&MT work contains just four steps. They are easily stated, but much more complex when put into action.

1. Define the problem.
2. ***FIND THE PART THAT CARRIES THE PROBLEM.***
3. Elicit the memories that are the foundation for the problem.
4. Neutralize the problem memories.

case is complex, requiring that we address a range of complicating variables, including, occasionally, an FS Part that refuses to show itself.

Visualizing a Freestanding Part

Locating and visualizing an image of the problem Part provides the most efficient means of conducting Parts work. Doing so allows your patient to recognize that the Part can be differentiated from the Conscious Self—the collection of Parts that present as a single entity in "patient" or "client."

Once you locate an FS Part, you should request that your patient describe the Part in some detail (e.g., with a description of its hair style, make-up, or facial hair, and especially the colors and styles of clothing, such as, "cut-off blue-jeans and a yellow T-shirt," or "grey hair pulled into a bun." This process helps in two ways: first, the process of description will likely bring the image into sharper focus for your patient, and second, your written description provides both you and your patient with a tool to find the Part again when memories fade a bit after a few sessions.

Although we can work with a Part without having an image of it—as when we work directly with a body sensation or an inner voice—I prefer to use an image whenever possible. It makes the work somehow more real—like working with things rather than working with a disembodied voice or a feeling without an image.

Requesting an Image.
The most direct way of acquiring an image of a Part is simply to ask for it. Once my patient has located the emotion or body sensation, I suggest that he speak to that state and request an internal image of itself. For example, I might say, "Speak to that sensation and ask it to give you a picture or an image of itself in your mind." I usually add, "You can speak out loud, or you can silently direct your thoughts to that sensation." Suppose he's unable to locate a body sensation. In that case, I suggest he speak to the emotion he experiences in the same way, requesting an image from that emotion wherever he experiences it.

A Mirror for the Unseen Part.
Sometimes an FS Part is shy, or anxious, or otherwise unwilling to show itself to the patient. A technique that frequently helps is to suggest to the unseen Part that it examine itself in a mirror because doing so will likely transmit the Part's image to the patient. If this doesn't work, then the Part is probably resisting. You can shift your focus in that case to the body sensation produced by the Part and interview by talking to the body sensation. Often, this tact will lead the hidden Part to communicate more openly.

Increase the Body Sensation.
The request's effectiveness can be improved by first attempting to modulate your patient's body sensations, perhaps a tightness in the chest, butterflies in the stomach, or a lump in the throat. The idea is to make the sensation

clearer to your patient and demonstrate that he is communicating with a Part of himself. I ask that he speak to the sensation "as if it were a person" and request that it increase the sensation's strength. If the sensation increases, as it does most of the time, I point out that this is communication with the Part that provides the sensation: he made a request, someone heard the request, and someone responded to it. Since it wasn't the Conscious Self that responded (because he is speaking for the Conscious self), it had to be a Part within him.

Often, at this point, an image of the FS Part producing the sensation may spontaneously appear in his mind. If not, having created the pathway for communication, your patient can now request that the sensation provide an image of itself (i.e., an image of the Part). Occasionally, there is a miscommunication here, and an image of an associated body part (e.g., heart, lungs, intestines) appears rather than the Part that causes the body sensation. No matter, you can communicate with the body Part as if it were a person-like Part.

Step Back, Step Forward.
This technique helps to find a Part by requesting that an emotion or body sensation first "step back," and if there is a response, then ask it to "step forward." For example, you might say to your patient, "Notice that sensation of anger [or sadness, or anxiety, etc.] and ask it to step back from you, or reduce its intensity." The intensity usually decreases. Then ask it to step forward, or increase its intensity. Regardless of whether it follows the suggestion, you've now

prepared it for further communication and for asking it to show itself to the patient as an image in his mind.

The 180-Degrees Switch.
Sometimes when you speak to an emotion and ask it to give you a picture of itself, you may get a picture of the person or circumstance that caused the emotion rather than the Part that feels the emotion. For example, your patient may want to work on his anger, and you have asked him to think of someone or something that will trigger mild anger as he sits with you. He might choose to think of his father to trigger his anger, but when you ask him to speak to his anger and request an image of it, he may get an image of his father rather than an image of his angry Part. (Confusing things further, occasionally the father might also be the image that the patient has unconsciously created to represent his angry Part. It's generally helpful in these cases to ask the angry Part to choose a different image for itself.)

Assuming that the father's image isn't also the image of the angry Part, you can guide the patient's angry Part (still blended with the patient) to switch places with the father's image (i.e., change position by 180 degrees). That would mean that the angry Part shows itself to your patient by taking the father image's position, while the father image returns to the patient's position viewing the scene. Your patient should now be able to view the angry Part.

Two Fishermen with a Net
The next technique often works when the previous ones fail. This approach is the "Two-Fishermen-with-a-Net"

technique. In this case, I suggest that my patient visualize herself in an open place and then:

> Imagine that two fishermen are walking past you, on each side of you, holding between them a tightly stretched, magical fishing net. It's magical because it can move through your body without harming you. As the fishermen walk past you on each side of you, the net they hold moves right through you. But it snags on and wraps around the sensation (or emotion) you feel. Then, as they continue to walk past you, the net pulls that Part of you out of you. And as the net emerges from you, gently place it in a nearby room. Then look into the room and tell me what you see.

She should now be visualizing the previously hidden Part, although sometimes the Part may be tangled in the net and not fully visible. If the image of the FS Part isn't visible, speak into the room and ask for the Part to show itself. If you cannot get a response, move on to a different technique or return to the body sensations you began with and use an affect bridge to locate early disturbing memories. Continue the therapy by focusing on the SIM Parts embedded in these memories and neutralize their painful emotions.

Other Variations in Freestanding Parts

There can be considerable variation in the organization of FS Parts. They may have few or many autobiographical memories or they may appear as child Parts, teenage Parts, or early, middle, or late adulthood Parts. They can even present themselves as older than the patient. A Part can look like the patient as she is now or as she looked at a different time in her life. It might not look like the patient at all or it might look like a cartoon character—a famous one or one that resembles the patient.

An FS Part might oversee a patient's full set of themed memories from childhood through old age. A different patient might also organize painful memories according to a common theme but his FS Parts might carry memories only within a certain age range. For example, the first FS Parts might carry the patient's memories up to puberty; a second Part might carry memories from puberty to adulthood at age 21; a third Part might oversee the patient's memories from the beginning of adulthood up to the present. Each of the Parts might look like the patient as he ages over his lifetime. And each of them them would be limited to memories of events within its age range and would have no memories of events of earlier or later age ranges.

Case Example.
A 43-year-old patient had an FS Part named Julie that held the patient's earliest anger-producing memories from childhood through the age of about 12. She had no later memories. Julie was replaced by Melissa, who carried the memories from early adolescence through high school graduation. During the patient's freshman year of college, Sandi became the new caretaker of anger-producing memories extending from college to the present time. Each Part acknowledged the existence of the other angry Parts but

denied knowledge of their memories. We worked with Sandi to heal the painful memories of adulthood. However, to heal the patient of her extreme, destructive episodes of anger, we also had to heal the younger Parts' memories.

Bridging to FS Parts from Known Parts.
Once you've completed neutralizing a targeted Part of its disturbing memories, you sometimes have an opportunity to work with another FS Part without returning to the full protocol. You may be able to bridge from the Part you neutralized to a new Part. You ask the first Part if it's aware of another Part that could benefit from our work. For example, suppose you have completed your work with an anxious FS Part. If this Part agrees to do so, you can request (through the patient) that she introduce or "bring over" the other Part(s) it knows. You can then continue your work by eliciting and healing the memories carried by the new FS Part(s). If you have developed a working relationship with this Part, you could even recall it on another occasion to help you search for a Part that's in control of the issue you want to treat next.

Types of Freestanding Parts

Most FS Parts can be typed through their functions, although such functions are not always easy to decipher—and not all patients have Parts with the same functions as Parts of other patients. In this section, I will try to hit on the major types of FS Parts that appear, but the list is by no means exhaustive.

Angry Parts.
These Parts are sometimes uncooperative when they first make an appearance, especially if you've had previous conversations with a patient who talked about getting rid of his anger or his angry Part. You may have to take some time to explain that you don't want to get rid of the Part or take away its power; you want to give it more power through helping it gain control over its own anger, meaning that it will cease being overwhelmed by its anger and learn how to use it selectively. You may have to remind it that when your patient rages out of control, so does the angry Part. You'll want to explain that everyone needs to be capable of appropriately expressed anger from time to time, but there is rarely a need for rage.

Angry Part Example.
For Barbie, a 27-year-old wife and mother of a toddler, the anger problem showed itself when she was overwhelmed by child and home care demands. Both she and her husband expected from her a high degree of efficiency. When the child's needs for attention interfered with cooking dinner or cleaning up the house, Barbie might scream at her husband for not helping her out when he came home from work—before disappearing into his den.

Or, if she were trying to clip the nails of her 18-month-old son, but his squirming and whining made it difficult to do so, she might scream at the ceiling—powerfully enough to hurt her throat and frighten her son.

We worked with angry Barbie by eliciting her painful memories and healing the SIM Part in each high-energy memory scene. The theme that best characterized the angry Part's memories was powerlessness in the face of Barbie's mother's micro-control of her life. An example of this was when, in the sixth grade, her mother forced her to give up her closest friends in favor of new ones that her mother found more socially acceptable.

Taskmaster Parts.
These Parts are the ones that bustle around the house and keep it straight, take care of errands when needed, or at work, rarely put things off until later, making the calls or writing the emails that keep her on top of everything. She's the one who makes reservations for vacations, schedules activities, and ensures that all family members have adequate packed clothes, devices, and toys.

Romantic and Sexual Parts.
We all have romantic and sexual Parts, but sometimes they are separate Parts, and sometimes they are blended into one. My experience suggests that they are more often separate, especially for women, but I haven't systematically studied this. What I find interesting is that romantic Parts often present themselves as teenagers, even when the patient is middle-aged.

Skeptical Parts.
Skeptical Parts seem to show themselves most often at the beginning of therapy when we present concepts and procedures new to our patients. The skepticism isn't just about the kind of work we do in Parts and Memory Therapy. It's a more general skepticism about the nature of psychothera-

py, regardless of the psychotherapy model. (I suspect this Part is active for patients in many contexts outside of therapy.) I try to greet skeptical Parts by congratulating them for demanding necessary explanations and for working hard to protect the patient. But I also ask them to "step back" and observe without interrupting while I guide the patient. I invite them to step in and raise questions but wait until I've shown them how everything works.

Addicted Parts.
Whenever a patient comes to therapy for help with an addiction, there's always at least one Part that specializes in keeping that addiction alive. The therapy begins with this Part. Addiction here refers to both substance or behavioral addictions, including alcohol, drugs, pornography and shoplifting. In each case, we first focus our healing work on the negative life experiences of the addicted Part; then, we carry out an additional set of interventions with the memories of the positive feelings that inevitably accompany the addiction.

Not-Me Parts.
It's common for a patient to occasionally have Parts that feel to her as if they are not her Parts. I call these Parts *not-me Parts*. It's useful to point out to the patient that everything in her head is her, and while a Part may feel like a not-me Part, it belongs entirely to her. It's just as real as other Parts with whom she feels a kinship. And as far as I can tell, after more than 20 years of observing Parts, there

is no significant difference in how we need to treat me and not-me Parts.

A Not-Me Example.
A few patients have difficulty with the idea of having me and not-me Parts. In one case, my patient balked when I tried to guide him in a neutralizing ritual with a not-me Part. He said that the Part would not release the negative emotions connected to the memory because he (my patient) didn't believe it would work—he felt that he had no influence with the Part.

The memory involved a complex scene in which my patient, when he was a newly adolescent boy, had his first sexual experience—partly coerced and harmful but also pleasurable because it helped him "feel more like a grownup." The intervention targeted both the negative and positive aspects of the experience. We neutralized the memory's negative energy because it was disturbing, and neutralized the memory's positive energy because it resulted from coercive actions.

I got permission from my patient to speak directly to the not-me Part to carry out the intervention. Then I asked the Part to listen to my voice as I recited a neutralizing ritual metaphor (because my patient balked at doing so himself). My patient left the session pleased with the results, but still perplexed that he could have Parts that didn't feel like Parts of him.

Parts in Dreams.
Some Parts seemingly appear only in dreams. But like other Parts, they can be contacted and engaged in conversation. Most of the time, dreams don't require interpretation. If you want to understand the meaning of a dream, the best way to do so is to ask the "dream maker" what it wanted the patient to know.

When a patient can see a Part of herself in a recalled dream, the Part she sees is often the Part that dreamed the dream. But with other dreams the dream maker is off-screen. In that case, you would ask the visualized Part to bring over and introduce the dream maker to the patient. You can then ask the dream maker what it wanted the patient to learn from the dream.

Case Example.
Cheryl, a 31-year-old patient with a history of sex abuse from age 3 to early adolescence, had frequent disturbing dreams about her abusers. She explained, "I dream, and I have conversations with the people who molested me. When I wake up, I feel scared—like I'm having a panic attack. In the last one, he introduced me to others as his sister. I wondered why he did what he did to me if he thought I was his sister."

Cheryl could clearly visualize and converse with her dream Part as it appeared in the dream. And although the dream Part wasn't also the dream maker, it knew the dream-maker Part. The dream Part agreed to introduce the dream-maker Part to Cheryl. It appeared to be about 12 years old, had its hair in a ponytail, and wore a pink dress. I coached Cheryl to ask the dream maker what it wanted to communicate through its dreams. The dream maker explained that it wanted Cheryl to reveal everything that happened to her as a child, including the identities of her abusers. "And she wants me to find myself," Cheryl finished.

The neutralizing work here focused on the anxiety, described by Cheryl as a panic attack, experienced by the first Part that appeared in the dream. Cheryl experienced the dream Part's panic when she awakened. The dream maker's suggestion that Cheryl share the stories of her abuse and abusers with the world-at-large would require further discussion, but the idea of revealing all was a part of the meaning of the dream.

I work similarly with nightmares: partially reduce the dream's negative energy by asking for clarification from the dream maker. Then complete the healing by neutralizing the fear experienced by the frightened Part—located either as a dream image or in the awakened patient's body sensations.

Critical and Punitive Parts

Critical or punitive Parts probably had a positive function in their beginnings, most likely by discouraging patients from taking chances or by encouraging them to conform to parental perfectionism. These were probably times when they had few defenses, and resistance would have caused even greater distress through harm to the body or emotional integrity.

In the present, however, these antagonistic Parts no longer function in a healthy way. We need to find ways around their harmful influence. Once the child reaches adulthood or has otherwise escaped the dangers of the original environment, we can disarm these damaging Parts through neutralizing their painful memories.

Killing Off Parts?
Patients will sometimes want to kill, destroy, or otherwise remove their intimidating Parts, but such Parts are built into the larger personality structure. Once created, they are likely with us forever. Fortunately, although the bundle of energy that we call a Part remains with us, we can transform it in several ways to become a positively functioning entity. We should carefully educate our patients about the nature of Parts and how we can transform them so that they don't make the mistake of hasty efforts to remove or kill them. That can slow down our work considerably as we fix the damage caused by such misinformed actions and rebuild trust with the affected Parts.

Case Example.
It's possible to visualize a Part killing or otherwise disposing of another Part. The patient might as a result be temporarily free of the offending Part. In one of my cases, there was a Part labeled "The Judge" who prevented almost all efforts to heal wounded child and juvenile Parts. One internal manager activated a Part called "The Hit Man." Unguided by me, my patient visualized The Hit Man going up to the Judge and shooting him multiple times with a hand-

gun. The Judge disappeared temporarily, but reappeared again within five days, still resisting the process of healing.

It might be possible to block a Part from interacting with other Parts for an even longer period of time. However, the apparently blocked Part would simply influence the patient nonconsciously and thusly become even more difficult to work with. It's much better to negotiate with an uncooperative Part in the clear.

Occasionally, a Part who has completed the neutralizing of all its painful memories, will have no interest in playing a new role in the system. Instead, the Part might indicate it was going on vacation or just going to relax on a beach indefinitely. In one case, a Part said to my patient that it was going to "tour the world." She watched internally as the Part walked away, waving goodbye.

Introjects.

Introjects are Parts unconsciously created by patients, which represent people who have been (and perhaps still are) influential in their lives. Usually, introjects form when a patient is young and relatively defenseless. However, they can appear in a person's life through at least early adulthood if the patient is still significantly affected by the person in question.

I've worked with patients who have developed parental introjects as late as age 20. Each of these patients constructed introjects at an early age, as well. Thus, some patients will occasionally develop several introjects, each representing the introjected person's perspective—as perceived by the patient at the time of the introjection.

The vast majority of introjects are representations of people who were threats to the developing child. My experience is that these constructs are most likely to form when the significant person—most frequently a parent or stepparent—posed both a continuing danger and was somewhat unpredictable as to when they showed either a negative or a positive side to the child. Introjects and their treatment are discussed extensively in Chapter 6.

SIM Parts

We can generally describe Stuck-in-the-Memory Parts as frozen in time, the time and place where the patient experienced what later became her long-term memory. They are also the first step in the creation of Freestanding Parts. FS Parts emancipated themselves from being stuck in singleton memories when repeated experiences (closely related in time or space, or with a common theme) called upon the SIM Part to expand its experiential base. The FS Part thereby frees itself from its singular moment to become the holder of a range of multiple moments (i.e., memories).

When addressed by the Conscious Self, a SIM Part is normally responsive in some way—a simple glance or smile, for example, demonstrates that the two entities (patient and SIM Part) are communicating. If they exchange further communication, they might even feel like they're having a verbal conversation. Happy moments such as weddings are good first choices when introducing P&MT because they illustrate that Parts' inner worlds aren't just about negative life experiences. Other high-energy, positive moments could include graduation ceremonies, awards presentations, births, and special birthdays.

Traumatic or painful memories often provide a sharper SIM Part image than positive memories. Still, I'm not eager to activate these Parts until I'm ready to proceed to the neutralizing interventions. That's because, once activated, traumatized SIM Parts may remain activated for some time, causing unnecessary emotional pain to our patients. This is especially true when they are activated near the end of a session and you don't have the time to center your patient before he leaves.

The Step-Away Technique.
This technique is useful to help your patient view a SIM Part from outside herself when the patient and the SIM Part are blended as one. The Conscious Self and the SIM Part view a memory scene through the same set of eyes, with the Conscious Self borrowing the SIM Part's viewpoint. We want the Conscious Self to view the scene as if she were standing outside of the SIM Part because it's less confusing for the patient than remaining blended in the memory scene and having to distinguish her own emotions from those of the SIM Part during the intervention.

To utilize the step-away technique, you begin by asking your patient (the Conscious Self) to describe the memory scene in some detail, and especially to find an object upon which to focus. Then you can guide your patient to estimate the distance between the object and her eyes. The purpose is to ground her in the setting. For example, if your patient can say she sees her brother standing about three feet away, she is well-grounded in the memory scene. Then, because both she and the SIM Part share the perception of her brother from the SIM Part's point of view, you can coach your patient to speak to a point directly behind her eyes (perhaps by tapping your (the therapist's) own head two inches back from the front of your head) and ask the SIM Part to take a step away from her (the Conscious Self). That should produce the patient's third-person view of the SIM Part. This exercise makes it easier to continue with the protocol and to eventually neutralize the SIM Part's negative emotions.

Recruiting a Memory-Scene Bystander.
Another technique to give the patient a third-person view of a blended SIM Part is to call upon a bystander in the memory scene. For example, in a remembered scene where the patient's mother punishes her, and her sister is watching, you could coach your patient to communicate with the sister image and request that she speak to your patient's SIM Part and ask that it step away from your patient. You would assume that the remembered sister can see both the SIM Part and your patient (regardless of whether it can or cannot). After the step-away, your patient should see the SIM Part in the third person in a way similar to the sister's view.

Chapter 4

Parts Dynamics

This chapter describes some of the essential tools and dynamics of working with Parts and Memory Therapy. The first two techniques, the "Step-Back" and "Twinning" techniques are temporizing or recentering techniques that may be utilized by both therapists and patients.

The Step-Back Technique

The "Step-Back" technique is a valuable tool at any stage of therapy. At the beginning of therapy, it can be useful in calming a new patient, anxious about meeting you or anxious about his own self-presentation. Later in therapy, among its many uses is in calming or shutting down a patient's eminent panic attack or other emotional intrusion into the flow of therapy. At the end of a session, it's useful in helping a patient become recentered if the session's work has left him with a residual of negative emotion. We want him to leave the office feeling calm and centered. Table 3 below describes the process.

Table 3. Protocol for the Step-Back Technique

1. Ask your patient to focus on her feelings of distress. Ask her to focus on where in her body she feels any negative emotion or body sensation, such as her teary eyes or chest tightness.

2. Ask her to speak to the emotion or sensation as if it were a person, and ask it to "Step back, but don't go away. Just step back." (No one likes to be told to go away, including Parts.)

3. Regardless of whether some relief follows the request, coach your patient to say, "Thank you, that helps. Please take another step back."

4. When the time seems right, point out that when you speak to an emotion or body sensation, you're speaking to a Part of the Conscious Self.

5. Following the second Step-Back, coach your patient to say "Thank you" once more, then request that the Part take two final, giant steps back, and then have a seat in the patient's personal auditorium–where she (the Conscious Self) occupies center stage and interacts with the outside world while her Parts influence her from the hidden auditorium in the inscape.

6. Guide the patient to adjust the Part's position in the auditorium from row 1 to 51, depending upon how far back from the stage it needs to sit to make the patient comfortable.

7. The patient should now be ready to continue the session from a centered place. The intervention aims to provide the Conscious Self with a continuing means to bring order to her inscape, moving Parts closer or further away as needed.

The Twinning Intervention

Twinning is an intervention aimed at bringing to the patient temporary relief from current-time stress, fatigue, or overwhelm. It's not permanently healing because it doesn't neutralize the memories that underlie the long-term problems in emotional functioning. I have found it useful to think of it as a means of clearing out the accumulation of negative emotions and body feelings resulting from difficult but not overwhelming everyday life. At the conclusion of this exercise, I want my patient to feel calm and centered, comfortable with facing whatever current challenge awaits in the near future.

Originally, I developed this technique for countering the fatigue my patients often felt after a session of neutralizing three or more emotionally demanding and disturbing memories. The Twinning technique restores lost energy and disposes of leftover negative emotions not successfully reached by earlier neutralizing work.

Later, I found that the technique also works well at the beginning of a session when a patient arrives at a session already emotionally triggered, perhaps after a night of bad dreams, the morning's domestic argument, or felt harassment at work. These sorts of problems can be gently put aside with the Twinning intervention, allowing our patients to focus on healing the powerful negative effects of trauma-like experiences from the past.

Table 4. Protocol for the Twinning Intervention

1. Explain that the Twinning will bring a few hours or a day or two of relative calm and peace and that permanent healing of major problems requires neutralizing memories.

2. Explain that you want your patient to visualize and create a temporary identical twin Part of herself to help her find relief from the day's stress, fatigue, or emotional upset.

3. To help your patient visualize her twin, describe aloud what she is wearing, the colors and styles, her jewelry, hair length, color and style, etc. Suggest that she should make room next to her for her twin to sit or stand. The only difference between the twin and the patient is that the twin is empty of all emotions or body sensations.

4. Direct your patient to examine herself from head to toe and wherever she finds any unpleasant emotions or body sensations, to lift them out of herself and hand them over to her twin for temporary storage in her empty spaces.

5. Guide your patient to visualize a waterfall (or a suitable substitute) in front of them and to walk into the waterfall with her twin. Ask your patient to speak to her twin and suggest that she feel how the waterfall soaks her hair and clothing and then flows through her entire body from head to feet, dissolving the negative emotions and body feelings and washing the cloudy water out of her, cleansing her to a state of calm and centeredness.

6. Suggest that your patient check her own body for remnants of negative energy she couldn't transfer to her twin and wash these remnants away. As long as she stays in contact with the twin, touching her hand or shoulder, the waterfall intervention should work for her too.

7. Guide the patient to bring the twin out of the water and store her inside for another day.

SUD and SUE Scales

A necessary means of discovering the significance of an autobiographical memory is to elicit a rating of how much negativity or positivity (actually how much not-negative energy) the event produces on a 0-10 scale. For this I use SUD (Wolpe, 1969) and SUE scales (Noricks, 2011). The SUD (Subjective Units of Disturbance) scale measures how disturbing, distressing, or painful something is. A score of zero means the memory is neutral. A score of 10 means that something is as distressing as it's possible to be.

The SUE (Subjective Units of Energy) scale measures how much energy is invested in a memory when that energy is not negative. For example, romantic love brings a positive energy; porn viewing is usually but not always positive; and sometimes a patient may have memories that are not easily classified as clearly negative or positive, just that they are somehow significant. The SUE scale is appropriate in such cases.

The use of these scales is essential to doing Parts and Memory Therapy because they provide an efficient means of assessing how well our interventions are working. They also provide us with the information we need to determine when the processing of particular memories is complete. Rarely is any score except zero an indication that we have finished our work.

When we elicit the SUD or SUE scores, we elicit them from the most relevant source. In most scenarios there are three entities involved—the Conscious Self (i.e., the patient), the FS Part, and the SIM Part that's frozen in time and experiences the same energy (SUD or SUE) that the patient experienced when the event occurred. It's not uncommon for each of the three entities to report a different score for the targeted emotional memory.

Case Example.
Barbie's case provides us with an example of differing weights for the same memory as experienced by differing entities. In one session, we had processed the pain Barbie felt in giving up several friends of whom her mother disapproved. In the next session, we turned to the memory of saying goodbye to one of her new friends—who moved out of state. At first, Barbie thought the memory was too trivial for treatment because it barely registered on her SUD scale (as the Conscious Self). She said she was "used to" losing friends now. However, we soon found that for the adult, angry FS Part, the memory rated an 8 on the SUD scale because her mother had set her up to be abandoned once again. Further, for the 12-year-old SIM Part that directly experienced the new loss, the memory rated as a 10. To ensure we're processing all the relevant memories, we must check SUD scores with the Parts involved (both FS and SIM) rather than depend upon the Conscious Self's offhand judgement.

I've found that checking patients' (i.e., Conscious Selves') SUD scores against their Parts' SUD scores is especially important for certain male patients who come to therapy for anger problems at the urging of their wives, but are unable to clearly see why their wives are troubled. They are likely to say they have no early disturbing memories (i.e., their SUD scores are zero for what we might view as very likely painful memories). They say things like, "I had a wonderful childhood, great parents, great family, great friends in school." If they stay on to do therapy, they may discover that the deaths of close relatives, the quarrels of their parents, or certain bullies in school were tough to deal with at the time. But they have done so well at dissociating their painful life experiences that they are honestly unaware of the continuing negative impact of them through nonconscious triggers and hidden Parts.

Adjusting Scales to the Part's Ability.
Sometimes the idea of an abstract SUD score is beyond the cognitive abilities of younger child Parts. Making a judgment about something on a zero to 10 scale is an abstract ability many children do not acquire until early adolescence. You can adapt the scale for use in these cases by asking the child Part to demonstrate the distress using hands to show their level of distress. Hands flat against each other would be zero while hands stretched wide would be 10. A 5 would be somewhere in the middle. In the few cases when a Part is unable to manage even this kind of scaling, you can still ask for an assessment of the energy attached to the memory by asking whether it's "a little bit," "some," or "a lot."

Getting a SUD (or SUE) score is very important to Parts and Memory Therapy for several reasons. First, getting the SUD score at each therapy stage, allows you to track your progress to zero. Ideally, you should be able to neutralize any given painful memory within 30 to 60 seconds. When the intervention takes significantly longer than that, you can expect to find either a manager blocking the work for its own reasons or an earlier memory that continues to amplify its distress onto the memory scene on which you work, replacing the negative energy as quickly as you neutralize it.

A second reason has to do with the science of memory reconsolidation. To prepare disturbing memories for neutralizing, we must reactivate the targeted memories, making them labile rather than seemingly indelible. Much of the time just locating the FS Part that carries the memory, and especially interacting with the SIM Part embedded in the memory, will accomplish that reactivation. But my preference is to take the additional step of eliciting a SUD score from the SIM Part as well. The SIM Part cannot do anything other than activate the targeted memory because it must assess the memory by experiencing it again to give it a SUD score.

A third reason is more professional than psychotherapeutic. Making SUD score notes that document where you began and where you finished permits you to review with your patient all of the various issues you worked with and for which you provided relief. This documentation is important because of the efficiency of healing with Parts and Memory Therapy. P&MT dispenses with the negative energy of earlier memories, and provides such a seamless connection between old and new understandings and insights, that patients are often unable to recall, without prompting, how painful their lives were before you began to heal their wounds. Because of the seamless reconnection of their life narratives, it often becomes difficult for them to recall how much you helped them and, unfortunately, they may significantly undervalue your work. And that's important for the future referrals that will eventually dominate your practice. In sum, use your documentation to remind your patients how powerful your work with them has been because they may come close to forgetting that they ever had the problems you helped them fix.

Patient VS FS Part in SUD or SUE Rating.
In using a SUD scale with a patient when not working with a specific internal FS Part, ask, "On a 0-10 scale, how disturbing is that memory to you now?" In the case of a non-negative memory (SUE scale), ask, "On a 0-10 scale, how positive is that memory for you now?" You could also ask, "How much energy is in that memory for you now?" while using the same SUE scale. The answer you receive will represent whatever emotional Part is dominant among those that make up the Conscious Self at that moment. Still, you won't know which Part provides the answer without further investigation.

There's an important difference when you wish to assess how a specific FS Part scales a memory. (The question becomes even more complex when you want an assessment from the Stuck-in-the-Memory [SIM] Part, but we will deal with that later.) In this case, you must be sure to direct your patient to ask the FS Part to answer the scaling question. For example, you would say to your patient, "Ask the Part to think about this memory now and tell you how disturbing (or upsetting, or painful, or uncomfortable, etc.) it is on a 0-10 scale." This step is crucial during the neutralizing process when you want to know how well a given intervention has succeeded. Unless you specify that you want the information from the Part, your patient may reply based upon his own assessment. Often an answer that comes quickly from your patient may indicate that he is answering based upon his own assessment rather than upon that of the Part. You should expect a short pause following your question while your patient checks with the Part.

A Part's SUD Score of Zero on a Next Memory.
When your patient locates the next memory to work with, and the FS Part he's working with says its SUD score for the memory is zero, it probably means that the memory was not an event in which the Part participated. Unless this Part worked previously with the memory, the Part was just an observer at the event, not an active player. You would want to seek out the Part that participated. Parts can be aware of a patient's life experiences without being involved in them; instead, they acquire information as observers rather than participants.

Angry Parts.
When working with the SUD score of an angry Part, initial attempts to understand how much distress an angry Part feels may produce a misleading answer. For example, suppose you had used an affect bridge to locate the angry Part's earliest significant memory, an event when someone beat your patient severely as a 5-year-old. Yet, when asked about the event, the angry Part may indicate no distress for

the beating. In a case like this, the angry Part is most likely not distressed because it didn't personally experience the beating. Instead, its anger follows from its role as protector of the child Part. It's angry because its charge was severely beaten. In such cases, you should reframe the SUD question so that it's about the angry Part's distress over the pain of the child it's protecting rather than a question about how the angry Part felt about being beaten as a child.

In sum, angry Parts acquire their angry energy in two ways. The first way involves the angry Part's protective response to the pain of a vulnerable other, as indicated in the previous paragraph. Autobiographical memories are the second source. Here, the angry Part is hurt and angry about events in which it was directly involved.

Checking the SUD or SUE Scales.
After the first pass of an intervention, you would check the Part's new SUD rating. Your patient might indicate that the distress level is not yet at a zero but has reduced, for example, from a level 9 to a level 4. To prepare for the next pass, you should frame your query in the form of "What makes it a 4 but not a zero?" In this way, you ideally acquire a new target for neutralizing, such as, "Now I feel guilty for not stopping sooner." You then ask your patient to ask the Part to focus on that guilt and once more carry out the intervention.

If you ask simply, "Why is it a 4?" your patient might think you're asking about the success of getting from 9 to 4 and then respond with something like, "Because I feel relief," or "Because I washed away the rest." This response is not a bad thing, just a misdirection. It doesn't give you a new target for further neutralizing.

The use of SUD and SUE scales are discussed again in Chapter 6. Some remarks may overlap with the material we've just covered, but it bears repeating in Chapter 6 because that's where we describe the process of neutralizing memories and the problems we face when doing so.

Parts Have Memories; People Have Parts

In working with recalled autobiographical memories, the P&MT model views all such memories as located within the memory sets of specific Freestanding Parts. Each FS Part has its own set of memories. Memory sets of other Parts may sometimes contain some of the same memories but no two Parts have exactly the same set of memories. If they did, one of the Parts would be redundant, making it likely that the two Parts would fuse into one. In fact, the technique of causing all Parts (or alter personalities) of patients with dissociative identity disorder (DID) to share identical memory sets was an essential step in the misguided process of fusing all alter personalities into a single entity as a means of healing DID. (See Cornelia Wilbur's work with the famous "Sybil" [Schreiber, 1973].)

The Conscious Self (i.e., the patient), is not the direct holder of memories. The individual Parts that make up the aggregate I call the Conscious Self collect the patient's memories and selectively share them with the Conscious Self through a seamless blending of Part and self. Thus, when a person (Conscious Self) shares memories, she is drawing upon the memories of whichever Parts are dominant at that time.

FS Parts Manage SIM Parts

Because they hold a person's memories, FS Parts also hold or manage the SIM Parts embedded in the memories. When we neutralize the painful emotions of SIM Parts, we often cannot carry the interventions to completion until we have secured permission to do so from the FS Part that holds the relevant memories.

SIM Parts are ubiquitous, numbering possibly in the hundreds, depending upon the number of high-energy moments a patient can recall. There is a SIM Part in every memory, and the vast majority of such Parts have only one isolated memory. The memories themselves are organized according to themes, so that different FS Parts manage different themes. SIM Parts are similarly organized according to the types of themes of the memories in which they are embedded. They are generally quiescent until inadvertently activated by a person's current-time triggers or intentionally activated by trained therapists doing memory work in the therapy room.

Freestanding Parts Manage High-Energy Moments.
FS Parts protect the Conscious Self by dissociating the high-energy of emotional memories into the nonconscious mind. In doing so, they reduce the intensity of the memories to a tolerable level, permitting the person to go about everyday life without being overwhelmed by the intensity

of the original circumstance captured in the memory. Imagine, for example, how difficult it would be for a child to manage day-to-day experiences if he continued to experience every day the initial intensity of a remembered bullying incident or the embarrassment of a teacher's scolding.

Or imagine how difficult it would be for an adult to experience daily the intensity of remembered trauma of war, or of being fired, or of learning that his spouse had cheated on him. High energy, positive moments would similarly create coping problems if their intensity is not reduced to a manageable level. Consider how difficult it would be to function if you remained intensely aroused by the joy of a wonderful 21st birthday or taking first-place in an athletic event or experiencing the birth of your first child.

Naming of Parts

Some Parts have their own names when we first interact with them (i.e., a name that differs from the patient's name). Other Parts choose names when first activated. Still others call themselves by the same name as the patient. Other variations are Parts who don't have names and don't want one, Parts without names who want one, and Parts without names who don't care if they have their own proper names.

Often the alternate names Parts present are childhood names bestowed by different relatives or nicknames favored by a group of friends. My sense is that the likelihood of Parts having names before we differentiate them positively correlates with childhood trauma (i.e., how often disturbing experiences activated these Parts).

Some therapists are uncomfortable with using names for discovered internal Parts. Presumably, this is because of their fear of reifying constructs by treating cognitive categories as something real when they are not. My view is that Parts are natural phenomena of the mind and that the reluctance to use Parts' names is a holdover from approaches that still insist that the mind is unitary despite overwhelming contrary evidence.

Additionally, it was once a guideline for therapists working with patients diagnosed with dissociative identity disorder to refrain from using names for alters since the ultimate goal of therapy was to fuse all alters into a single entity. Using names for alters would reify as something substantial what should best be understood as a temporary abnormal condition. Further, the "self" in such fused cases would in theory have no awareness of any Parts of the self, even under hypnosis (Kluft & Fine, 1993). Implicit to this conception of the self is the related assumption that having Parts of the self is somehow abnormal.

Once you interact with Parts and discover that they do indeed have personalities and agendas of their own, you'll find that the naming fear is unfounded. Parts are already real. Naming Parts helps therapists and patients remember which Parts they are working with or have worked with previously.

Most Parts have the same names as the patients and prefer to continue to use those names during our interactions. When Parts have the same name as my patient, I find it helpful to designate them with their name plus their age, such as Sally 14, James 22, or Tina 6. Often, I simply call them "the 6-year-old" or the "14-year-old" or simply "22." If you are uncomfortable with using proper names for Parts, you might feel comfortable referring to a Part by some action it claims as its own, such as "the Part who played hooky" or "the Part who protects young Parts." However, when such ad hoc descriptions become too wordy, it might be more efficient to identify them by their presenting ages.

Sometimes a patient will resist using her name for her Parts. Jenny was one of my patients who objected to calling one of her child Parts, "Jenny 8." She said that she felt "uncomfortable" doing so. But she was okay with calling it "the child Part in a red dress." Jenny also resisted the temporary separation of Parts from the self for healing, even after successfully doing so. She insisted that it was "not logical" to do so. Clearly, she had a Part resistant to the new way of understanding self and mind we were introducing. Eventually, I convinced this "logical" Part to separate from the Conscious Self so that we could continue with the work of healing without interference.

Do Parts Lie?

Parts can lie and mislead you and your patients, but they seldom do so. In a recent case, one of a patient's three angry Parts lied about being the one that raged at the man's wife a few days earlier. In two other cases, I learned about previous lies when my patients returned to therapy after some time away. In both cases the lies were that the SUD score for memories being neutralized had reached a zero when they had not. Other instances involved misleading me about whether the Part was acquainted with other Parts I asked about, such as "the Part who avoided sex with her husband." Rather than lie, most Parts will instead remain silent. I suspect that most cases of intentional misleading aims to protect more vulnerable Parts from discovery.

In one case, Andrew, a 48-year-old married man, returned to therapy after a two-year absence because his marriage had deteriorated to the point that both he and his wife agreed they should return to therapy or get a divorce. They also both agreed that he was always angry. After concluding our second set of sessions, the angry Part expressed how much better it felt about Andrew's wife. It went on to share that it understood now how important it was to neutralize painful memories completely, and it wished it had done so two years earlier. It admitted that it had lied to us when it said Andrew's painful memories were at a SUD level of zero—it thought it needed to keep some of the pain so that it could better protect Andrew.

Ages of Parts

Freestanding Parts may develop as young as age two or three, and theoretically they could form in old age, but that would imply that the elder faced a situation for which none of her existing Parts had a solution. New Parts appear when existing Parts are unequipped to handle novel challenges. And it's why most Parts appear in childhood and adolescent years—when new demanding life experiences are frequent.

It's important to remember that images of FS Parts, as they present themselves to patients, are generally symbolic, although the meaning of the symbolism may be obscure. A Part may present itself as a cartoon character or a line drawing, a physical object such as a ball of fire, a cloud, or a shapeless blob, or even a monster, a religious figure, or a demon. So, when a Part presents itself as an older person but claims an age of 7 or 8, we should not be surprised. A Part might even claim the age of 100 when the actual age of the patient is 37. Or a Part could present its image as 37, the same age as the patient, but claim an age of 8. Tentatively, until your interviews suggest otherwise, you could hypothesize that something significant happened when the patient was 8 or even that despite its 37-year-old costume, it continues to view the world through the eyes of an 8-year-old.

Sometimes an FS Part, especially in a managing role, will mistakenly believe that the patient we are working with is still a child. For example, it might assume the patient is still 7 years old—the patient's age in the memory we were planning to neutralize—rather than the actual adult age of perhaps 35. In such cases, correcting the age perception may be necessary to gain the manager's cooperation in therapy. Otherwise, it might insist that the patient was still in need of the precautions inherent to keeping painful memories unchanged. Once the manager understands the patient is an adult and no longer in danger it will generally cooperate with the therapy.

Conversations with Parts

As a therapist, when you communicate with a Part, the conversation works best when you talk with the Part through the Conscious Self. While it's often possible for you to have a conversation directly with the identified Part, with the Part speaking through the patient in the first person as "I," this inadvertently encourages Parts to take executive control of the body from the Conscious Self. Having direct conversations with a Part works against a major goal of the P&MT model. Specifically, we want to strengthen the position of the Conscious Self as the system manager while reducing the tendency of well-intentioned Parts to speak for the Conscious Self in times of stress.

The same reasoning applies when we work with patients diagnosable with dissociative identity disorder (DID.). In this extreme version of Parts organization, individual Parts may take full executive control of the patient, leaving amnesia by the Conscious Self for whatever occurred during the time of executive control. We want to encourage blending and coconsciousness between Parts and Conscious Self rather than Parts' full executive control, which would produce amnesia in the Conscious Self.

In interacting with the Part through the Conscious Self, you coach your patient how to talk with the Part. For example, initially, you coach her to ask a new Part stabilizing questions such as, "Ask the Part if it knows who you are;" "Ask the Part who it is; "Ask the Part if it knows it's a Part of you." By doing this you subtly guide the Conscious Self to take charge of the conversation while also training the Part to communicate with you through her as well.

When Emotion Overwhelms the Interview.
During this early stage of familiarization, when you, the patient, and her Parts are still learning how to communicate with each other, it sometimes happens that the distress level of a Part threatens to overwhelm the Conscious Self, perhaps with anxiety or with tears. Or, it could be an observing Part (i.e., a Part not directly involved in the interview) who is so affected by the emotions triggered in the targeted Part that it begins to overwhelm the Conscious Self with similar anxiety or tears. You can usually calm the patient by asking her to speak to the targeted Part or to the distressed observing Part, and ask it to "take a step back" and then another step back as needed. This step serves the purpose of calming the targeted Part enough to continue with the interview. Or, if it's an observing Part getting in the way of the conversation, the request to step back, especially coupled with an assurance that you will soon talk with that Part too, allows you to acquire the space you need to proceed.

Trauma with a SUD Score of Zero.
Sometimes, a patient will claim no distress regarding a once-traumatic or otherwise painful memory—something that she dealt with before seeing you. You should judge that assertion with skepticism. This might happen if she has done a significant amount of cognitive or other mainstream therapy that merely drove (dissociated) the emotional memories into the nonconscious part of her mind. But after you've helped her

reactivate those memories, she will see that her emotional memories are incompletely healed after all. You can then carry out neutralizing interventions as usual because your work is informed by the SUD scores of FS and SIM Parts, not by the SUD scores of the Conscious Self. In such cases, it may help keep her engaged with the therapy to ask the relevant Part to "come closer" to the Conscious Self so she can feel some of the emotion felt by the Part. In this way, her doubts about still-distressing emotions are quelled, and she is now more committed to the interventions that will follow.

Avoiding Too Much Blending.
Although it can be helpful for the patient to feel some of the emotion felt by a Part in distress, you don't want her to be too close to the distressed Part. Too much blending between Part and patient can interfere with the therapy. In the following example, my patient Sandy and I worked through a large number of traumatic memories of childhood abuse. She was driven by her taskmaster Part to accomplish as many interventions in a session as time permitted. This Part also insisted that the Conscious Self should experience the SIM Part's pain in the targeted memory. As Sandy said, "I can't ask my Parts to experience pain unless I'm willing to experience the pain too."

It's interesting here that even after more than a year of work with Parts of many kinds, Sandy failed to recognize that this noble insistence upon sharing the pain (she was talking about the pain of memories of years of rape and torture) was also Parts-driven. The Part was blended so seamlessly with the Conscious Self that Sandy thought of its characteristics as part of her own character's essence rather than the expression of a devoted helper Part.

The downside of Sandy's big-hearted view was that sometimes grief overcame her during the therapy with bouts of sobbing that left her temporarily unable to speak, which required us to pause our work to help her become centered again. Another problem was that her powerful emotional response to the traumatic material also activated other less-involved Parts, causing them temporary overwhelm and making it difficult for Sandy to be calm at the end of the session.

To ease our way to continuing the therapy without undue discomfort for Sandy, I confronted the taskmaster Part, reframing its function as "therapy helper," and got its agreement to "step back" from the Conscious Self and permit me to be the leader in carrying out the therapy. Helping a patient to avoid this kind of overwhelming affect is the primary reason to work with a wounded Part at an emotional distance from the Conscious Self. It's also one of the most significant benefits of Parts therapy: Our patients don't have to reexperience the original trauma to heal.

When a SIM Part Is Unresponsive

When working with a disturbing memory, the patient may visualize himself in the memory. However, this visualized SIM Part may be unresponsive to his efforts to communicate and be unwilling or unable to participate in its own healing. The first option would be to work with the FS Part that holds the memory in its memory set. If this option is unavailable for some reason, you may be able to neutralize the memory despite the initial lack of cooperation by the SIM Part.

For example, in one case, an adult male patient I will call Frank could visualize his childhood self in a remembered scene in which his parents were loudly arguing. Frank believed that he was frightened during that event, but could not identify fear or any other emotion connected to his parents' fight. He could visualize his 7-year-old SIM Part staring at the parents. But the child Part was unresponsive to Frank's efforts to establish communication. Finally, after explaining to the immobile image that he, Frank, was the boy now grown up and ready to help, he asked the Part to notice where in its body it felt its fear or other strong emotions. Then, as I narrated the intervention, Frank visualized a powerful wind blowing through the SIM Part's image and carrying away as tiny particles of dust all the negative emotions it felt as it watched Frank's parents argue.

When Frank now asked the SIM Part how disturbing the painful event was, it responded for the first time by raising its hand to waist level and rocking it back and forth in a gesture Frank interpreted as meaning, "So-so." Because that seemed to be more than a SUD level of zero, we repeated the wind intervention. Following that repeat, the Part shook its head no when asked if there were any other bad feelings attached to the memory. Frank said that he felt relieved of the unpleasant sensations he had not previously noticed. He indicated that the Part also looked relieved. Frank added that the SUD score was now zero.

Chapter 5

Elicit the Memories that are the Foundation for the Problem

Autobiographical memories represent the foundation and the focus of our work in Parts and Memory Therapy. They are the early sources of present-day problems and the continuing sources of everyday problems as well. Neutralizing problem memories is the most powerful intervention we have for the healing of our patients. In doing Parts and

---

Table 5. The Parts and Memory Therapy Protocol

The basic protocol for all P&MT work contains just four steps. They are easily stated, but much more complex when put into action.

1. Define the problem.
2. Find the Part that carries the problem.
3. ***ELICIT THE MEMORIES THAT ARE THE FOUNDATION FOR THE PROBLEM.***
4. Neutralize the problem memories.

Memory Therapy, you will discover that nearly every negative emotion, sensation, attitude, or belief held by your patient has a clear origin in life experiences recorded in his autobiographical memories.

Introducing Patient and Part

In preparation for eliciting autobiographical memories, you will want to spend some time developing a relationship with the newly differentiated FS Part. But before that, you want your patient to describe the Part: human or nonhuman, apparent gender and age, and how the Part dresses, along with the colors of its clothing. If the image is nonhuman, then collect a clear description of the blob, cloud, ball of fire, monster, etc. The purpose here is to familiarize both you and the patient with the Part's appearance, so that you can more easily find it again if needed.

When ready to communicate with the Part, I generally request that my patient ask the Part if it knows who the patient is. The most frequent response is yes, although a minority of Parts don't immediately know her. Even when the Part indicates that it knows the patient, you should verify that by requesting the patient to ask the Part what is its belief about who the patient is. It's not unusual to find that the Part views the patient as a friend, a sibling, or a parent.

Once the Part accepts that the two of them are somehow the same individual, and the Part correctly identifies your patient as "Susan," for example, you will want Susan to ask for additional get-acquainted information. You have a lot of flexibility here in finding the best language and approach in guiding the patient to interact directly with the FS Part.

I usually encourage my patient to ask if the Part knows her father, mother, spouse, children or other significant people in her life. Further, I suggest that she ask whether the Part considers these significant people to be *its own* father, mother, spouse, etc. Sometimes, the Part denies knowing these others. And sometimes, even when the Part acknowledges awareness of these significant people, it may deny having the same relationship with them as does your patient. For example, an angry Part might acknowledge that Bill is Susan's husband, but not the angry Part's husband. This sort of finding that a Part may have different relationships with relatives or friends than does the patient, helps the more skeptical but observing FS Parts to realize that Parts are real and have their own minds and world views.

Additional get-acquainted questions might include the age or felt-age of the Part, how old the Part believes your patient to be, whether the Part has the same name as your patient or any name at all, and whether it wants a name if it doesn't have one. When a Part insists that it doesn't want a name, an age designation for the Part will usually be enough for you (and your patient) to recall the Part in later sessions. For example, the "six-year-old" or the "12-year-old" can be sufficient.

Eliciting Memories

With the orienting questions asked and a cooperative relationship established, it's time to begin eliciting the FS Part's autobiographical memories. With a few exceptions—such as porn episodes, the remembrance of past romantic loves, or the highs of habitual drug use—the memories we work with are painful in some way. When you're prepared to elicit memories, you guide the patient in asking the FS Part to share its earliest disturbing memory. At this point, you're prepared to systematically elicit and neutralize the FS Part's full set of disturbing memories, from earliest to latest.

I assume that the earliest action memory (as opposed to static scenes without people or animala) is the one that brought the Part into being. If the memory we initially find is not the earliest, it's still likely to have the same emotional theme as the earliest memory, which means that we can use it at as our starting point for neutralizing.

Parts appear in response to critical moments in a patient's life. For this reason—understanding the patient's life-shaping events—the earliest memory has a greater importance than others. But if at first, I cannot initially find the FS Part's earliest memory, I'll settle for any painful memory regardless of its recency. Once the process of recall has begun, other memories earlier and later—linked by a common theme—will soon appear.

There was a time when I wondered if my questions might be creating artifacts. I thought that by asking for the earliest disturbing memory, I might unintentionally be causing my patient (and his FS Part) to locate a memory that would confirm my hypothesis that disturbing or other high-energy moments created Parts. For this reason, I would initially ask for the Part's earliest memory of any sort (i.e., positive, negative, or neutral).

As time passed, and the same pattern continued of painful or other high-energy memories appearing as the earliest memories, I eventually began asking directly—in the interest of efficiency—for the earliest disturbing memory. On the occasions when the first memory cited by the FS Part wasn't disturbing, it seemed to be general background or a typical, emotionally neutral scene.

Such innocuous memories are not the same as high-energy, positive memories. Positive memories sometimes become problems, too. For example, drawing upon a case about which I've previously published (Noricks, 2011), parents lavishly praised their four-year-old daughter for her help in moving from one home to another, as well as her continuing eagerness as she grew up to help parents and sisters with their family chores. However, the helper Part created in childhood became a problem for the grown-up child in adulthood. She became an attorney and repeated her pattern of helping others ahead of herself. The junior attorneys and paralegals she helped praised her helpfulness and generosity, but her neglect of her own work caused her to be fired.

Objections to Emotion Words.
I often use the word "painful" as a general term in place of "disturbing" to include any emotionally negative expe-

rience. When a patient or FS Part balks at using this or another emotion term, insisting that the word doesn't apply to them, I will explain that we are looking for any negative experience, including disturbing, sad, uncomfortable, unpleasant, difficult, problematic, or troubling memories. The point is to elicit memories that should be neutralized and not to define too precisely the emotions we are targeting.

Significant Versus Painful Memories.
Sometimes there are situations where asking for your patient's earliest significant memory is more useful than asking for your patient's earliest painful memory. This is especially so when working with food issues, addictive behaviors, or romance. The problem memories may actually be positive, or your patient may be unable to say whether the memory is positive or negative, just that the experience was significant. In these cases, the 0-10 SUE (Subjective Units of Energy) scale will measure both the initial level of significance and the level to which the memory is reduced due to your interventions. Note that what is significant should be determined by your patient.

When Memories Are Missing
A few patients are initially unable to link a given negative emotion or body sensation to specific memories. The most efficient way to get beyond this seeming impasse is to proceed with the neutralizing intervention as usual, guiding your patient to bring wind, water, fire, or something else to dispense with the negative emotions. As your inter-

vention begins to erode the negative emotions, what will most likely happen is that relevant memories will flash through your patient's mind as the intervention cleanses them.

Another circumstance that might initially appear absent of disturbing memories occasionally appears soon after you've located an FS Part. The Part may be unable to recall any memories at all. When you encounter this situation, remember that all Parts have memories. Without memories, Parts would not exist. It's unclear why this phenomenon presents itself, but it's generally easily fixed.

You would address the FS Part through the patient as usual and ask—adjusting to the age of the patient—"Do you remember going to high school?" With the expected answer of "Yes," you then ask whether life was perfect at this time of his life. It's impossible to answer this question without accessing consciously available memories. If high school life wasn't perfect, then you can ask for an example of an imperfect experience. You could repeat the process with middle school, elementary school, and pre-school ages. Even if the FS Part is mute, whatever comes to your patient's mind necessarily comes from the Part because the two of them are locked together in a cognitive-emotional embrace. Whatever the patient says derives from the FS Part.

Using this approach will also give you a rough estimate of when the Part first appeared in the patient's life—because the appearance of the Part marks the beginning of its memories.

Child Parts May Have Adult Memories.

The Freestanding Part's presenting age doesn't prevent its acquisition of experiences that happen later than the Part's presenting age. For example, one female, 28-year-old patient had a 14-year-old FS Part that functioned to manage emotional abuse experiences through silent unresponsiveness. These experiences continued into her late teen years and were included in the 14-year-old Part's set of themed memories. The Part had memories of silently endured emotional abuse as late as age 18, when she moved out of her parent's home. What seems to be happening is that the presenting age of the Part indicates the approximate age when the Part first appeared in the patient's life rather than the age when memories are capped.

Chapter 6
Neutralize the Problem Memories

Neutralizing the emotional energy attached to autobiographical memories is the most powerful, permanently-healing intervention we can offer to our patients. We accomplish this by focusing on the Part that carries the problem, and then on the memories that maintain the problem from within that Part's themed set of memories. Then, we

---

Table 6. The Parts and Memory Therapy Protocol

The basic protocol for all P&MT work contains just four steps. They are easily stated, but much more complex when put into action.

1 Define the problem.
2 Find the Part that carries the problem.
3 Elicit the memories that are the foundation for the problem.
4 NEUTRALIZE THE PROBLEM MEMORIES.

---

neutralize the emotional memories (not the factual, autobiographical memories) by visualizing the disappearance of the painful emotions through water washing them away, wind blowing them away, fire burning them up, or any other action that symbolizes their permanent absence.

Only recently have we learned why certain of our interventions have worked so well. I refer here to what I now call "neutralizing" (Noricks 2005, 2011) and before that the work of two important influences of P&MT: Richard C. Schwartz's (1995) "unburdening" intervention and Helen H. Watkins's (1980) "silent abreaction" intervention . They worked well because we were unknowingly utilizing the universal process of memory reconsolidation, by which animals revise memories once thought to be indelible.

The pioneering work of Bruce Ecker and colleagues (Ecker et al., 2012; Ecker, 2020), in translating neuroscience findings into psychotherapy now permits us to claim a robust, recognized scientific basis for the success of our neutralizing interventions; viz. memory reconsolidation. This concept allows us to neutralize implicit emotional memories without significantly altering the explicit factual memories of traumatic and other painful or high-energy experiences.

Memory Reconsolidation

As Bruce Ecker and colleagues (Ecker et al., 2015) state, "Emotional memory converts the past into an expectation of the future, with or without awareness...." From a trauma scene's conversion of a traumatic event to an expectation of the future, the next step is to provide interventions that do not match that expectation. When we activate memories, and provide a mismatch between the expectation for continued trauma and the counterposed intervention of visualized relief, the memories are edited and neutralized.

Neutralizing Memories with P&MT

Directly neutralizing the SIM Part is more efficient than neutralizing it through the FS Part in whose memory set the memory is located. The FS Part and the SIM Part frequently express different ratings on their 0-10 SUD scores, such as 6 versus 8. Neutralizing the SIM Part's SUD rating from 8 to zero can usually be counted on to produce a zero also for the FS Part. But neutralizing the FS Part's SUD rating of 6 to zero may leave some of the SIM Part's distress unprocessed.

Processing the FS Part's Memory Set

I've found that processing painful autobiographical memories is most efficiently handled when we can work through the FS Part. We elicit a memory, neutralize the emotional energy of the SIM Part embedded in the memory, and return to the FS Part after each intervention to elicit the next disturbing memory. Once we've established good communication between therapist, patient, and the two kinds of Parts, the therapy generally proceeds rapidly to the point where all the FS Part's significantly disturbing memories heal.

With many patients, however, therapy doesn't proceed in an ideal way. Sometimes an FS Part cannot be located, and consequently there's no facilitating manager with which the patient and therapist can interact. Most often the reason for the Part's apparent absence seems to be shyness or fear of the unknown. Still, the hidden FS Part is likely to be monitoring our progress as we engage in a work-around to continue the therapy.

The Affect Bridge.
One work-around involves an affect bridge (J. Watkins, 1971). With this technique the patient focuses upon an emotion or body sensation while searching her past for the earliest disturbing memory that comes up. After neutralizing the emotions carried by the SIM Part in the first memory, we return to the original emotion or body sensation and repeat the process. The major drawback to continuing in this fashion—without an identified FS Part—is that we can't be sure we've located all relevant memories contained in the unseen FS Part's memory set. Fortunately, the previously unseen FS Part often shows itself as we continue working with the affect bridge.

The FS Part's Image.
In other cases, it turns out that the FS Part had not yet developed an image for itself. However, as we bridge to significantly more recent memories, we find an apparent SIM Part that begins to function also as an FS Part, and the image the FS Part takes for itself may be an image of the current-time patient, even dressed the same as him as he sits in your office. The key to recognizing this change in function is that the newly recognized FS Part will have a range

of memories over time rather than the single memory of a SIM Part.

Unseen Parts.
Another complication can arise when both the FS Part and the SIM Part are unseen. It's not uncommon for a patient to recall a memory in which she cannot view the SIM Part in the third person; that is, she cannot see the Part from the front, behind, above, or its side. Instead, she recalls the memory scene as viewed through the eyes of her younger self (the SIM Part) who directly experienced the event. We know that a SIM Part is present because the patient can describe the scene in considerable detail. Of course, we also know a SIM Part is present because without the presence of an observer (the SIM Part), there is no memory.

When the Conscious Self (patient) views a memory scene through the eyes of the SIM Part, there are several ways to help her view her SIM Part in the third person, thus making the memory processing more efficient (see Chapter 3). In a few cases, though, even these techniques will not bring the desired internal picture of the SIM Part to your patient. Nevertheless, we can still find a way to carry out a neutralizing ritual.

Neutralizing Unseen SIM Parts

One technique is to guide your patient to try to start a conversation with the SIM Part with whom he shares the view of the memory scene. Ask him to address the spot two or three inches behind the place he subjectively feels his observing eyes to be (i.e., the center of the head or brain). He might say, "Hi, I'm a later version of you, and I've come to help you out." Assuming that he gets a response, he could continue with standard orienting statements or questions: "Would you like to stop hurting? Would you like to have things work out differently? How old are you?" Often this initial conversation between Conscious Self and blended SIM Part will by itself spontaneously produce a visual differentiation of the SIM Part from the patient, thus providing him with a third-person view of the SIM Part.

Suppose the SIM Part is still unseen after your orienting questions have opened a channel for communication. In that case, you can encourage your patient to ask the blended SIM Part to focus on where its pain or other disturbing sensations or emotions are located in its body. Then you can bring the neutralizing imagery to bear on the SIM Part by directing the patient's intervention toward the spot where he imagined his blended younger self to be. For example, in one case I suggested that my patient imagine a leaf blower in the hands of a bystander in the scene—he could create one if a bystander is not already present. Then I coached my patient to direct the bystander to send the leaf blower wind through both the patient and the blended SIM Part to carry away the negative energy. In this case, the patient's Conscious Self was both a part of the target and manager of the intervention to neutralize the reactivated memory. Another way to do it would be to guide the patient in stepping into a waterfall, while directing the water toward the SIM Part's sense of its body. At the same time, you could remind the Conscious Self that he too was in the water and he might be able to wash away any residual negativity that the SIM Part failed to manage.

In the second case, my patient wanted to heal the remembered pain of lost love he had experienced many years before, when his high school girlfriend broke up with him. The break-up scene was that of his girlfriend telling him she didn't love him anymore, and then walking away down an empty school corridor. He had already reactivated the memory and located the same powerful pain he had originally experienced. He could not separate the SIM Part because of his powerful sense of being fully present in the school corridor. I suggested that he visualize a very powerful wind blowing through him and the now-empty corridor as it carried away the unseen SIM Part's pain of loss. The intervention was successful.

The necessary element in these examples was the reactivation of the original memories in such a way that the patient fully reexperienced the original pain. Without this element, the interventions would not have had any effect.

Unblocking Therapy Blockers

Many FS Parts initially object to neutralizing the emotional memories contained within their own memory sets. Reasons for such objections include fear of change and fear of the unknown. They need assurances that their fears are unfounded. Before beginning an intervention with a given memory, it's always a good practice to request permission from the FS Part whose set of memories you're going to utilize. Otherwise, you may have to do so a few minutes later when it blocks your efforts to begin the intervention.

Angry Parts.
Perhaps because angry Parts are generally the most powerful Parts in a system, they are more sensitive to potential threats to their positions than are other Parts. They may block interventions not just within their own memory sets but also within the memory sets of Parts they consider essential to the patient's functioning. For example, a common but false belief among Parts is that a painful lesson learned requires holding onto some of the pain if the lesson is to be retained. A parallel false belief relates to holding onto the grief of losing a close relative: if you no longer grieve a deceased person, you will forget them.

The Two-Step.
In addition to asking permission from the blocking Part, angry or not, there are several other techniques available to us. I've found the most important of these is the "Two-Step" neutralizing intervention. This technique requires bargaining with the blocker. In step one, you would coach your patient to assert to the blocking Part that she can demonstrate that what the Part fears will happen, won't happen. Such fears might include losing the wisdom of a lesson learned, beginning to forget a loved one, or the blocker becoming weak or beginning to disappear. This demonstration involves the SIM Part filling up a container (supplied in the patient's imagination) with all of its memory's negative energy (i.e., physical pain, sadness, fear,

grief, etc.) and keeping the container in its possession. The blocking Part would then assess whether any of the feared consequences appear to be happening. (Note that we treat emotions and sensations as if they were physical objects when we talk about putting them into a container. Within the inscape, the world in which you can have conversations with Parts of the self, this doesn't matter. Within the inscape we can treat imaginary objects as tangible objects.)

In step two, the blocking Part would ideally recognize that its concerns were groundless and then would permit the intervention to continue, releasing the emotional energies to wind, water, fire or some other symbolic cleansing. This is the result in the vast number of cases—because there is no downside to neutralizing painful emotional memories. Nevertheless, a blocking Part will occasionally object in the second step.

In some cases, the blocking Part will take a middle road, not requiring that the negative emotions be taken back inside the SIM Part but choosing to keep the contents in the container until it feels it's safe to dispense with them. In such cases, I generally suggest that the blocking Part permit the SIM Part to "place the container on a shelf" or that the blocker place the container on its own shelf until assured that its concerns were unfounded.

There is actually no problem when the blocking Part retains the container. We have already neutralized the SIM Part's memory. Placing the emotional memories in an imaginary container on an imaginary shelf is just as effective as using imaginary wind, water, or fire to neutralize them. Even with the two cases I've seen where the blocker reneged on the bargain and directed that the container contents be taken back inside the SIM Part, I've found that the memory in question is no longer a problem at our next therapy session. Evidently, visualizing the removal of the SIM Part's emotional memories before returning them to the SIM Part will suffice to neutralize them. The intervention produces enough of a mismatch between the original memory's implicit expectations and the brief removal of emotional pain into a container that memory reconsolidation permanently seals the neutrality (see Chapter 1 on mismatches).

Punitive Parts.
A judgmental or punitive manager might block the neutralizing of a SIM Part's pain because it believes the patient is guilty of wrongdoing. This manager feels that the patient should be punished with continued suffering. The punitive Part might be unaware of how much time has passed since the patient committed the presumed crime., and, like SIM Parts, may itself be stuck in time. When shown that the patient is no longer a child and that 10, 15, or more years have passed, the punitive Part may grudgingly agree to permit the intervention. It can be helpful to point out that even second-degree murderers often get out of prison within ten years.

If you can't convince the punitive Part to permit the intervention, you could ask about its history of painful experiences. If it agrees to heal some of its disturbing memories, and you have shown it the benefits, it will generally become flexible enough to stop blocking your original intervention.

If not, the "unmasking" intervention, sometimes required for "introjects," described elsewhere, may be necessary.

Anxious Parts.
Sometimes a patient comes in with a heavy load of daily anxiety that prevents initial work with Parts of the self. I find it helpful to use that anxiety to introduce Parts and Memory Therapy. I will point out that the anxiety represents the presence of an anxious Part, and we can reduce it by speaking to the anxiety the patient feels in her body and asking it to "Step-Back" (see Chapter 4). Then a second Step-Back request should further reduce the anxiety. That should produce sufficient muting of the anxiety that the patient's metaphor of being center-stage in her auditorium will permit her to place the anxious Part at a comfortable distance from her among the seat rows in the auditorium.

We should now experience a more relaxed patient, permitting us to continue with the plan for the day. Or, if the anxious Part has provided an image of itself, we could begin work toward neutralizing the memories that produce the anxiety. Sometimes, repetition of the Step-Back technique over two or three sessions may be necessary before introducing neutralizing interventions.

Skeptical Parts.
We expect skeptical Parts at the beginning of therapy. That's understandable since Parts and Memory Therapy is unique and relatively new; most members of the general public are unfamiliar with it. There are overlapping areas with other therapies, such as those that recognize Parts,

subpersonalities, voices, ego states, etc. And there are now a few other therapies that recognize the power of memory reconsolidation. But patients who have previously worked with standard talk therapies are likely to have no experience with Parts or memories as Parts and Memory Therapy utilizes them.

My approach is to bring skeptical Parts into the conversation. I welcome them and urge them to continue their work. But I also ask them to be patient, permit me to carry out my interventions, and examine the results before rejecting the therapy. If possible, I also like to use the skeptic's voice as a means of drawing Parts into the conversation. For example, I might ask my patient to speak to the skeptic's voice or the feeling of skepticism, and request that the Part show itself. If it does so, the scenario provides us with a great stepping-off point for becoming acquainted with and working with other Parts of the self. I've found that by making an ally of the skeptical Part, the therapy flows more smoothly than if I argue with it.

Neutralizing SIM Parts

Although we elicit memories from Freestanding (FS) Parts, we generally direct the actual healing intervention at the Stuck-in-the-Memory (SIM) Parts. That's because the SIM Part is the entity that directly experienced the targeted memory. An FS Part has been emancipated from any single memory but oversees its entire set of memories in which SIM Parts are embedded. An FS Part enables the patient to experience less and less emotional pain over time by partially dissociating individual memories from consciousness. Consequently, the SUD score for a given emotional memory is likely to be less for a patient's initial rating than it is for the FS Part that stores it. Sometimes, dissociation of the pain is complete and the patient will insist that the memory doesn't bother him. A bit of investigation will quickly demonstrate this as a false belief.

Further, the SUD score for the same memory as experienced by the Stuck-in-the-Memory (SIM) Part is always greater than or equal to that of the FS Part. That's because from the SIM Part's point of view, the memory is current-time, lived experience, not a memory. With possibly a dozen or more other memories that constitute its memory set, the FS Part usually feels a greater emotional distance from the targeted memory and gets a lower SUD score than the SIM Part. This concept is consistent with the FS Part's function to dissociate high-energy moments into the nonconscious mind. Consequently, the Conscious Self often rates his level of distress as less than that of the FS Part for any given memory. In the extreme case, because of the FS Part's efficiency in dissociating a memory's pain, the Conscious Self might insist that the memory rates a zero on the SUD score. In a case like this, we might have to beg the patient's indulgence while showing him that the memory continues to generate negative emotions even when the patient is unaware of it.

In my first P&MT book, *Parts Psychology* (Noricks, 2011), I chose to work first with the FS Part when neutralizing painful memories. It seemed reasonable to do so because what I called an FS Part was widely recognized as the

Part, subpersonality, ego state, voice, side, etc. that other scholars worked with. Working with the FS Part appeared to be sufficient to produce a SUD score of zero for the memory. Only if we incompletely neutralized the memory, would I guide my patient to work with the SIM Part (which other scholars either didn't recognize or merged it with the FS Part as a single entity). Further, I occasionally found that reducing the FS Part's SUD score to zero didn't always mean that the SUD score for the SIM Part would be zero as well.

The reverse is not true. When we work first with the SIM Part and reduce its SUD score to zero, the FS Part will also achieve a SUD score of zero—unless there is interference from an out-of-sight manager or an intrusion from an earlier memory into the FS Part's space.

Neutralizing with Metaphors

We change an FS Part's emotional memories forever while neutralizing the pain of the SIM Part embedded in each of the FS Part's disturbing memories. And we forever change the FS Part's relationship with its past. Beginning with the FS Part's earliest disturbing memory and working through its entire set of disturbing memories right up to the present, we turn off the energy that powered the negative emotions of each memory. In its place, there is only neutrality and calm. The explicit, autobiographical memories (i.e., factual history) remain largely unchanged, including whatever wisdom the patient has acquired through experiencing the remembered events. The FS Part and the patient will also not forget that the now-neutral emotional memories were once painful.

The neutralizing metaphors we use to guide our patients in healing are limited only by therapists' and patients' imaginations. The essential element is that whatever your patient visualizes should involve a metaphor of permanent release. I quote below three examples from my book, *Parts Psychology* (2011). These are fairly rich metaphors, but simpler ones can also work quite well. For example, one of my patients found that all she needed to do to neutralize her emotional memories (e.g., sadness, fear, shame) was to wrap them into a ball and "throw them away." Another said, "Let's flush them down the toilet." I like the more elaborate rituals because they make it easier for patients to grasp the concepts. They provide an elaborated descriptive picture of the process that is easier to visualize than to simply, "toss the negative emotions into the trash."

I've found it particularly helpful to suggest to my patients that as wind, water, fire, or other imagery transform them, the memories become like black and white text in a boring history book—factually correct but devoid of emotional content. And like a history book, the explicit memories continue to provide the wisdom of accumulated life experiences.

Water Intervention

Visualize the Part as standing in a waterfall and notice how sometimes there are drops of water and occasionally mist and sometimes powerful pouring.

Let the water flow over, around and through it. Notice how the Part's hair plasters to its head and its clothes stick to its skin. Ask it to locate where it stores the problem memory within it and then ask it to feel the water dissolving the pain and negative emotions connected to the memory. Notice how the negative emotions dissolve in the water as the water washes them out of the Part. You may even notice how the water around it is discolored as the dissolved negative emotions wash away. As the water continues to wash away, the Part's anger [or fear, sadness, etc.] you may notice how it gradually becomes clear again as the memory is washed clean.

Fire Intervention

Visualize a bonfire for the Part and ask it to stand nearby. Then ask it to locate where it is within itself that it stores the painful memories. Now ask it to reach inside of itself and lift out those negative emotions and throw them into the fire. As the fire touches them, they burst into flames and incinerate the emotions. Ask it keep repeating the action until the fire entirely consumes all of the negative emotions and sensations attached to the explicit memories. (A popular alternative is for the Part to dance in the fire while burning up its negative emotions.)

Wind Intervention

Visualize the Part standing in an open field as you bring up a powerful wind to blow over, around, and through it. Ask it to locate where it stores the memories within itself and ask it to feel the wind scouring the memories and cleansing them of fear [or sadness, shame, etc.]. As the wind breaks up the fear into tiny particles of dust, you may notice that as the wind blows away from the Part it's darker because it's blowing away the particles of those emotions like dust or sand. Let the wind continue to blow until the memory is just a neutral memory with no emotion attached

Once a negatively experienced foundation memory has been neutralized for a given Part, we will never again have to work on that memory with that Part. Another Part that carries the same memory might require some work, but the work we did with the first Part is permanent. For this reason, following the neutralizing ritual, the only acceptable SUD score for a problem memory is zero. If the SUD score is greater than zero, we have not entirely neutralized the memory. You should continue to neutralize with one or another intervention until the SUD score is zero.

The Hurricane Intervention

Frequently, you may find that you cannot process a given memory to a SUD rating of zero through ordinary, simple interventions, such as wind, water or fire. Additionally, the SIM Part might not know what prevents the SUD rating reaching zero.

In these cases, before looking for a blocking Part, I suggest one last effort to process the remaining SUD with a powerful intervention. This effort is the "hurricane intervention," with category 2 hurricane winds of 100 mph. You would guide your patient to visualize a steel or concrete-and-steel post in the memory scene and then provide the SIM Part with enough rope to tie itself to the post so the hurricane won't blow it away. The patient gives the rope to the SIM Part, putting it in complete charge of the rope in order to avoid an accidental triggering of unknown memories of being forcibly tied up.

You would then direct your patient to prepare to carry out the intervention and nod to you when he is ready to go. You explain that with his nod, you will say, "Go!" and will count aloud up to ten seconds as the he blasts the remaining level 2 SUD energy from the SIM Part. Thus: "One, two, three, four, five, six, seven, eight, nine, ten, done!" The SUD score should now be zero. If, after this dramatic finish, the SIM Part still reports some negative energy remaining in the memory, you should look for the source of the blocking rather than continue battering away at the residual SUD content.

Blocking of Neutralizing

When simple interventions with a SIM Part fail to produce a SUD or SUE score of zero, that usually means another Part is blocking the therapy, which could be by intent or by accident. Check first with the FS Part that carries the memory. Acknowledgement may be the only thing it wishes, just the patient's request for permission to neutralize the targeted memory before action is taken.

Introjects

The most frequent blocker is a parental introject, especially an introject representing the dominant disciplinarian in the family. There can be more than one parental introject of the same gender, with different introjects created at different times in the patient's life. Usually, when you coach your patient to request permission from the introject to carry out the intervention, that's enough to be able to proceed. In more complex cases you may have to "unmask" (see below) the introject and heal the younger Part that wore the introject's costume.

Perpetrator Introjects.

A different kind of introject is one that represents the perpetrator of childhood abuse. This type of introject is most likely to interrupt the neutralizing process when the memories under treatment are memories of abuse. A simple request for permission to proceed is usually not enough. My experience has been that the most efficient way to move forward is to unmask the perpetrator Part. As with the results of other unmaskings, you will find that the Part that wore the costume now needs some neutralizing of its own pain before you can return to your original target.

Problems with Focus.

Sometimes a patient has difficulty focusing on the current intervention, with the result that she says the memory has disappeared, or the SIM Part has disappeared, or she has a flood of memories that prevents her from concentrating on the task we have begun. The problem could be the result of another Part intentionally blocking her concentration. In that case we have to track down the source to work out a solution.

Concentration problems could also result from the patient being overwhelmed by current-time problems, such as family or work issues. In such a case of unintentional blocking, depending upon your assessment of your patient's needs, you could try to fight through the distractions by asking the patient to direct the intervention out loud, or break off from the planned intervention while you take a session to stabilize the patient's current-time issues.

Overwhelming Trauma Scenes.
A trauma scene may be so overwhelming that it serves as its own block to neutralizing. The trauma may be so shocking, mesmerizing, or physically painful that we can't get the attention of the SIM Part long enough to carry out the neutralizing intervention. Examples of such scenes could include torture, rape, murder of another person, or a vicious beating. To heal such atrocities, we might first have to move the SIM Part to a safe place.

The Rescue
In one case, the trauma scene was that of a mother beating her six-year-old son with a thorned branch of a tree as it screamed and bled and begged its mother to stop. When I could not get the boy's (SIM Part's) attention, I directed the 25-year-old patient to imagine himself going into the scene and physically carrying his visualized childhood self outside the house. From there, we could guide the SIM Part in

releasing its pain, sadness, and fear. The process of removing the SIM Part from the trauma scene to a safer place is called a "rescue."

I prefer to limit my interference with the memory scene to the minimum amount necessary for neutralizing, as with the rescue above. But you could coach your patient to rescue the SIM Part to a completely different environment for a safe place. The location would depend upon the patient's life experiences. She could visualize the SIM Part's safe place as located in the time of the trauma, the present time, or the future. She could choose a relative's house, her childhood room, Disneyland, or a fluffy cloud in the sky. What's important is that the SIM Part feels safe from any threats that might be generated in the traumatic scene while also avoiding possible new threats in the new scene.

Rescuing isn't generally sufficient to thoroughly neutralize the negative experience, but it usually provides considerable relief to both the SIM Part and the patient. In this safe environment, you can reduce the SUD score of the emotional memory to zero.

Removing Blocks with Narrative.
Eliciting a narrative from the SIM Part, explaining the source and context of the traumatic event can also be helpful, including a statement about emotions experienced. This technique is especially applicable when the first pass or two of wind, rain, fire, etc. fails to reduce the SUD score significantly. However, when the SIM Part's additional information has no effect on the SUD score following another pass of the intervention, there is likely a

specific blocking FS Part you have to locate and negotiate permission to continue.

A similar technique would be to guide your patient to ask the SIM Part that began with a SUD rating of 8 and is now stuck at a 5, "Why is it a 5 now and not a zero?" We want to redirect the intervention based upon additional information. I've added the "...and not a zero," because leaving it at "Why is it a 5 now," will more likely generate a response of "Because I let go of some of it," rather than indicating what remains unfinished.

Typically, the answer will identify a given emotion such as sadness or anger or a belief like the phrase, "I can't do anything right." You can then repeat the intervention with the focus on the newly identified emotion or belief. I would follow the same procedure whatever the source of the remaining distress, whether it's an emotion, a belief, a circumstance, or even a sense of a Part's inability to articulate the issue. Thus, "Focus on that emotion or belief and let the wind blow it away."

Interventions Blocked

I've found just two sources for blocking of neutralizing interventions. Sometimes, in working with what we believe to be the earliest painful memory, we discover that there's another, still earlier memory that's being triggered and amplified in such a way that the Part we are working with is picking up the amplified pain. We cannot reduce the SUD score of the later memory to zero because the earlier memory's broadcast of pain replaces the pain attached to the later memory as quickly as we remove it. The solution is to find the earlier memory, and its SIM Part, and neutralize that emotional memory first. Taking the SUD level of the earlier memory to zero will probably result in a SUD score of zero for the later memory as well, given that we will already have done considerable work with the later memory.

The second blocking source also involves another Part in the system. In this case, there's an FS Part, a manager of some sort, with its own agenda blocking the intervention. Frequently, all we have to do is find this manager and ask its permission to continue our work. In other cases, the manager may object out of a fear that neutralizing the memory will reduce its power and its ability to carry out what it believes its role to be. The Part might even believe it could disappear if we carry out the intervention.

Example of Blocking by an Earlier Memory.
The problem arises when we haven't been able to find the earliest painful memory of the subpersonality with whom we are working. The solution is to find it now and neutralize it. An affect bridge from the Part we are working with to the patient's still-earlier memory will usually lead us to the disturbing memory we need to heal.

As the following example shows, it's sometimes challenging to find the earliest memory. My patient, a forty-year-old man who wanted to do his part in avoiding the hours-long arguments that punctuated his marriage, accepted the idea that we needed to begin with the earliest memory of problems with his wife. He focused upon the negative emotions he felt during his most recent argument and asked the Part with the emotion to show itself to him. What came up was a picture of himself at the age of 25. When he asked this Part for its earliest memory, he recalled a four-hour argument with his wife when he was 24. The Part had no memories of high school age or earlier. However, it did have a memory of a telephone argument with a different girlfriend at age 19 when he was overseas in the army. That memory had a SUD score for him of less than 1. I disregarded it at the time.

We spent almost all of the next session trying to neutralize the 4-hour argument with his wife. We were unsuccessful. I looked for blocking managers in as many ways I could think of but could find no blockers. The 25-year-old even refused the Two-Step intervention (described near the beginning of the chapter), which by its nature has no downside.

Finally, I suggested that my 40-year-old patient ask the 25-year-old Part to connect him with his "boss." I was looking for a manager. The Part immediately bridged to an image of my patient as a 19-year-old in his army uniform. This Part's earliest memory was the breakup with a girlfriend—the young woman in the telephone argument noted above—which I initially ignored. The 25-year-old Part didn't remember breaking up with the girlfriend and rated the argument as disturbing only at a level 1. But for the 19-year-old Part the SUD score was a painful level 9 for the breakup. We quickly neutralized the breakup memory. Once we neutralized that memory, we had no difficulty neutralizing the negative emotions from the first extended argument with the wife at age 24. We could not complete this work with my 40-year-old patient until we neutralized a different argument with a different woman 21 years earlier.

Blocking By Managers.
Managers come in many forms: an older Part that has assumed a protective role for a child Part; a perpetrator Part that functions to cause another Part to continue to suffer fallout from abuse experiences; system managers that resist virtually any intervention to bring change—usually out of a sense that healing distressed Parts will weaken or cause the manager to disappear; and more.

Other managers may be positive or negative introjects, demons or monsters, shadowy characters reluctant to show themselves, or a range of hurt Parts that closely resemble the patient in physical appearance, but at different ages of the patient's life. Success with moving forward in the therapy requires negotiating with managers, sometimes healing them of their own hurts, and sometimes transforming them from hostile introjects to hurt child Parts.

Working with Blockers.
The first step is to find the blocking Part. Most often all it takes is to suggest to your patient or her Part to look around the internal scene of the intervention for another Part. It might be a Part nearby, such as a mother introject standing by as the patient processes an injury caused by the mother or the Part might be an unclear image on the periphery. You can ask the mother introject if it's the one

blocking the work. You might ask the image on the periphery to come closer and then ask the same question of it.

When no blocker is visible, you can request that the blocker show itself. Or you can ask the Part if it has a protector, a manager or a boss—then bring the blocker into the scene. You can sometimes locate a blocker by asking the targeted Part to feel the resistance to the intervention and then to backtrack the resistance to its source and visualize it.

Asking Permission.
Sometimes blockers hide but will still respond if you ask permission to heal the Part in question. Sometimes a Part will not show itself and will not respond to a permission request. Sometimes you can get a yes or no response if you speak to whatever body sensation your patient is feeling during the conversation, such as tightness in the chest, anxiety in the stomach or a lump in the throat.

In the absence of an initial no-response from a blocker, you can again ask your patient to speak to the invisible blocker and state that he is asking for a yes or no to granting permission to neutralize the relevant emotion. Further, you add that the absence of a response will mean that permission is granted. That should either bring out the blocker if it objects—in which case you would negotiate with the blocker for its cooperation—or if there is no response, you may be able to complete the intervention without further blocking.

Negotiating with a Blocking Part.
Most of the time, just asking permission from the blocker is all that's necessary to complete the intervention. But sometimes more negotiation is necessary. In that case the best procedure to follow is to find a way to praise the blocker for its strength, wisdom, commitment to protect, etc. You can never praise a blocker too much. You want to develop rapport with the blocker. You might emphasize the blocker's role in protecting the Part or in helping the outside patient.

Some blockers have painful life experiences of their own, and you might have to do some healing of those memories before you can work with the first hurt SIM Part. You will want to emphasize that the blocker is the boss and that you are helpless to do the healing without its cooperation. The Two-Step intervention will almost always gain permission to carry out the intervention if other negotiations fail.

Asking the Blocker to Join the SIM Part in the Ritual.
Sometimes you can disarm a potential blocker by inviting it to participate in the intervention, perhaps joining the SIM Part in the water or the wind or at the fire. It might just give itself the same treatment the SIM Part gets, or it might help the intervention by encouraging or showing the SIM Part how to let go of negative energy.

Blocking by a Patient with a Zero SUD Rating.
Sometimes your patient will question why you want to work with a memory that doesn't bother him. One answer is to point out that this is a good sign that normal dissocia-

tion is working (i.e., that the FS Part has stored the emotions away so well that the patient can't feel the original distress at all). However, checking with the FS Part, and especially with the SIM Part, will demonstrate that the memory is still nonconsciously disturbing.

(Parenthetically, my experience has been that male patients are more likely to assert that what were once disturbing memories are no longer so. They may assert that the events were too long ago to hurt anymore, or they may assert that they have already worked through them with previous therapy. But in either case, we should doubt the assertions. Time does not in fact heal all wounds, although it can lead to dissociating them. And unless the previous therapy involved memory reconsolidation or extinction therapy, it's unlikely that the memories are neutral. Standard talk therapy will not neutralize trauma.)

Blockers Insisting the Part Should Suffer.
This is a variety of persecutor Part. It might present itself as a parental introject, or as an abuser from the past, and sometimes it may be difficult to discern its origin. The first two Parts can be dealt with through an unmasking. For the third, the best way to proceed is to try to get the Part to share its own earliest disturbing memory and following that with one or more neutralizing rituals.

Introjects and Monsters

Introjects are visual constructions in a person's inner world (the inscape), usually originating during childhood, that capture significant characteristics of people important in the person's life. Most often, parents or their surrogates are introjected. For example, an angry father introject might display impatience or sharp, angry comments. At the same time the father's nurturing or supportive characteristics might be absent.

Influential persons in a child's life seem most likely to be introjected when they are unpredictable in their anxiety-producing actions. When the person upon whom the introject is patterned, combines unpredictability with physical or emotional abuse, the result is a fertile environment for the appearance of introjects. By creating an introject of an abusive person, the patient carries around a ready reminder to be alert when that person is nearby.

Supportive Introjects.
Occasionally, a patient might introject positive characteristics of a significant person and thereby create an ego state that's nurturing and helpful. There was a positive father introject in a recent case whose only function appeared to be to provide companionship to a toddler Part. There was no need to unmask that introject.

In another case, a patient developed a manager Part to supervise and look after the system's child Parts. Its character and personality were based upon specific positive strengths of the patient's mother. As perceived by the patient, its image was that of the mother and it identified itself with the mother's name. Nevertheless, this positively motivated introject recognized that it was a Part of my patient and not the actual mother. Changing the mother image was unnecessary.

When positive, supportive introjects appear, I leave them alone. I think we can all benefit from a gentle hand of love in our inner worlds. But most introjects present us with problems in the therapy, primarily through blocking our neutralizing interventions. They slow down our work and sometimes require considerable negotiation before we can again move forward with the therapy. Still, as long as we can eventually gain their cooperation, I prefer not to unmask them.

Introjects Claiming Autonomy.
More severe problems with introjects appear when they refuse or are unable to acknowledge that they are Parts of the patient; instead, they insist that they *are* the person after whom they are patterned. Introjects of this sort will have memories of the same events as our patients, but the memories will be distorted to reflect the presumed point of view of the introjected person.

For example, one set of memories a child Part might carry is the mother's chronic physical abuse. The Part may be hurt and confused about why the mother treated it in such an unfair way. But the introject may view those same memories from the mother's purported perspective of having provided corrective discipline to an unruly and ungrateful child. These could not be the mother's actual memories because everything in the patient's head is his own. Instead, the purported memories from the mother's point of view can only be suppositions and assumptions of the patient about how the mother must have viewed the remembered events in question. They are just guesses made by the patient as a child in an effort to make sense of his mother's actions. They might or might not accurately represent the mother's point of view at the time of the incidents. In cases like this, the introject should be unmasked, as described below. Otherwise, the patient will continue to struggle with the conflicting views of his childhood history.

Neutralizing an Introject's Memories.
In theory, we could neutralize the distorted memories of a parental introject as we do the memories of other Parts. In practice, however, the work is quite difficult and confusing. At the outset, attempts to neutralize the presumed memories of the introject are inconsistent with the healing protocol. Neutralizing aims to heal a Part of its disturbing emotional memories. However, an autonomous introject presents itself as separate from the patient, presumably carrying its own load of disturbing memories referring to the offenses of the child. Although it's possible to play along as if the parental introject were the actual parent, and to accomplish a certain amount of weakening of the introject's inflexible position, more often attempts to heal the introject lead to confusion or wasted therapy time.

Unmasking Introjects and Monsters.

After many hours of frustrating work with introjects, I found that the simplest and most efficient way to work with problem introjects is to unmask them by asking them to remove their parent (or other) costumes. We can then heal the revealed younger Part that wore the mask.

The Unmasking Ritual.
Unmasking an introject by directing the hidden child Part to remove its costume is routine in Parts and Memory Therapy. I guide my patient in doing this only when the introject blocks our work and refuses to cooperate in healing my patient. I could speak directly to the introject and guide it to give up its false identity, but because I want my patient to become comfortable in managing her Parts, I will urge her to direct the unmasking herself.

In the passage below I provide a ritual narrative for the patient to use in guiding the introject's unmasking. I say or read a few lines at a time, pause as she repeats them to the introject, and continue in this manner until the instructions are complete.

> *Thank you for helping me to grow into adulthood. Because of you I've succeeded in surviving through difficult times. Congratulations on a job well done! Without you, I could not have survived. You are absolutely the best at what you do. Congratulations also on being the very best actor ever. And you've played a very difficult and exhausting role. You played the role of being my mother, and you convinced all the other Parts that you are her. But you can retire now, because you've succeeded in your job. You've guided me into adulthood. Thank you. You are wearing a mother costume but you are not my mother. You are me, a younger me. It's time*

now for you to take off your mask and costume and just be the younger me behind the mask and under the costume. So please just go ahead and unzip the costume and step out of it or pull it over your head, and let me see the me behind the mask.

Therapist's Unmasking Ritual.
Sometimes, my patient is too hurt or angry to say the positive things I suggest he say at the beginning of the ritual, especially that of offering thanks for the help in growing up. In these cases, I will speak directly to the introject on behalf of my patient. The following is a step-by-step guide for the therapist to carry out the unmasking intervention.

Table 7. Guide to Therapist's Direct Unmasking of Introjects
1. Thank the introject for helping your patient to survive into adulthood.
2. Congratulate the introject for excelling in its role of protecting your patient's health and life.
3. Assert that the introject has accomplished its task, and it's time to take a less demanding job.
4. Switch focus and praise the Part (usually a child Part) wearing the introject's costume for being an outstanding actor—perhaps the greatest actor ever—but it's time now to retire from its exhausting role.
5. Direct the younger Part beneath the costume to unzip the costume and step out of it or pull it over its head and *be* the younger [name of patient] beneath the costume.

> 6. Neutralize the negative emotions of the newly released Part.

In Step 6, you can generally heal the Part that wore the introject costume by neutralizing one, perhaps two, of its memories. Such role players rarely have more than two distressing memories. You can then return to the memory initially blocked by the introject.

Unmasking Monsters.
The process of unmasking monsters is the same as that for introjects. You substitute the monster for the introject in the treatment ritual. Monsters can take many forms and are not always a problem for the patient. When they are not a problem, there is no need to unmask them.

In working with a 24-year-old patient I will call Michelle, we ran up against a well-meaning monster that blocked us from neutralizing Michelle's distress over repeated sexual molestation from preschool age through her teens. We were preparing to neutralize the distress of her rape at age 16, when the monster appeared. Michelle described it as "huge, gigantic!" It was a giant blob, black in color with stubby legs, no arms, and a pointed head. It wanted us to stop therapy altogether because our work was making Michelle vulnerable to greater hurt. It reasoned that it had already placed Michelle in a safe zone by keeping her unhappy and resigned to her fate of continued unhappiness and powerlessness. By continuing to be in pain she would be protected from greater pain because it was something she expected; she would be less shocked and less damaged.

This concept is a common but false belief held by many blockers and other resisting Parts that initially refuse permission to neutralize disturbing memories. In fact, later trauma and loss will hurt just as much for the already-hurt Part as a not-hurt Part.

We negotiated with *Blob*, as Michelle called the monster, over an entire session to try to convince it to examine Parts we had already worked with and see that they were now no longer in pain. We offered the Two-Step intervention to show Blob how the intervention would work. We emphasized that Michelle was not a child anymore and at age 24, she was equipped to protect herself from new trauma. Blob could not be convinced; it was steadfast in its insistence that ending therapy was what Michelle needed. Michelle should continue to suffer now to prevent even greater suffering later.

The unmasking was reasonably routine except that even after the unmasking ritual, Blob managed to retain its costume until I asked for volunteers from a crowd of observing bystander Parts. Several of these Parts joined our effort to successfully remove Blob's costume, thus releasing the Michelle actor beneath the costume. After we had neutralized the central trauma of the Part that previously wore the Blob costume, we were free to move forward and neutralize the rape Michelle experienced as a teen. (Note that with P&MT, hypnotherapy is unnecessary. When working within a person's inner world, all you need is imagination and visualization.)

Clinical Example of an Introject's Complexity

In this example, I worked with a patient I will call Lucy to reduce her anger toward her husband. She called her angry Part *Blackie* because it was dressed in black. Its earliest disturbing memory was, surprisingly, a memory we had neutralized some months previously. When this happens, it's a sure sign of interference from a blocking Part—because once neutralized, a memory will never require direct neutralizing again. We then looked for blockers that might have pushed the distress back onto the Part we had already healed.

The memory was that of Lucy at 11-years-old, screaming and rolling about on the floor as her father kicked her. In this memory Lucy was the SIM Part. Her mother was in the kitchen, urging her husband to continue kicking Lucy. Looking around the memory scene, Lucy soon found a mother introject that admitted pushing the level-10 distress back onto Lucy after we had initially healed her. (Note that the mother in the kitchen is not the mother introject; she is Lucy's mother as recalled in Lucy's memory of the incident. Lucy created the mother introject unconsciously as a child, probably because the mother had such a powerful influence in her life.)

At first, the introject resisted our request to permit the child's release from punishment. But then it assented when I shared the information that the punishment of the SIM Lucy had been ongoing for more than 40 years now (Lucy was in her 50s).

After we checked that the SUD score for the 11-year-old was again a zero and we had stopped her father from kicking Lucy, we went ahead and unmasked the introject. Interestingly the mother costume just floated to the floor without an appearance of the usual actor-child Part in place of the introject.

At this point Lucy expressed that she still wanted an apology from her living mother, now in her 70s. I explained that an apology in the outside, everyday world would not heal the child's hurt in the inside, emotional world, where memories are real and still emotionally active. I suggested that Lucy instead reinflate the mother-introject costume like a balloon and ask that rejuvenated mother to apologize directly to the child in the memory. She did so and Lucy then deflated the mother costume once more. She no longer needed an apology from her 70-year-old mother.

Age Progression

Sometimes complex cases require us to go beyond our standard healing protocols to be more creative in our healing interventions. Age progression is a technique I borrowed from hypnotherapy for occasional use in P&MT. Its use permitted us to move past the blocking of our efforts to neutralize my patient's inappropriate sexual interest in children.

I will call my patient "Mandy." She had an early history of sexual abuse by multiple perpetrators from approximately three until puberty. One result of the chronic abuse was the creation of a large number of child Parts, as many as two dozen, each with its own experiences.

The second consequence of Mandy being sexualized at an early age was that some of the child Parts adapted to the abuse by accepting it as something positive, which they then attempted to introduce to other children in the outside world (to the great shame and guilt of the adult Mandy).

At age 25, Mandy found that she was attracted to children and insisted that these attractions be neutralized. We sought out the Parts with sexual interests in children and began healing them of their inappropriate inclinations. We accomplished this by systematically neutralizing the abuse memories of each affected child Part we could locate. We neutralized both the negative emotions of unwanted sexual contact and the positive sexual feelings that sometimes co-occurred with the negative.

Then we ran into a group of three eight-year-old Parts that banded together to prevent further neutralizing. Mandy had told them they had to give up their sexual interests in children because "it was gross" and that she was only interested in other adults. The child Parts responded that sex with adults was gross and there was nothing wrong with them being interested in kids their own age.

Unable to budge the three Parts from their position, we decided to age progress them to young adulthood, expecting them to adapt their sexual interests to persons of their own age. Mandy had only talked to them as voices until this point because they refused to provide her with individual images of themselves. But for Mandy to guide them in our planned intervention, I suggested she ask each of them to represent themselves by the color of their shirts. They chose pink, blue, and white. Mandy observed, "They look like triplets, wearing the same outfits, just different colored shirts."

With a stronger sense of her connections to these Parts, Mandy began the age progression intervention. I had first confirmed with her that she had memories that stretched from early childhood to her present age. The next step was for Mandy and the three Parts to clasp her hands and those of each Part so that they achieved a set of interlocking eight hands through which Mandy could share with them significant aspects of her life.

She touched on high points from late elementary-school-age onward, primarily memories of social relationships both in and out of school. The process took about 30 minutes as Mandy shared her memories and noted the three Parts' growth in body size.

Puberty and her first period were important, beginning at age 11. Other snapshots involved the first day of 9th grade high school, and the continuation of body changes as the young Parts grew and filled out their frames. A driver's learner's permit was important to Mandy at 15, as was getting her actual driver's license at 16. Her first boyfriend and breakup at 17 was memorable, as was her high school graduation. Finally, there was part-time work and part-time college through age 19 and then 20.

I described this intervention as if Mandy had memories of her own, but memories are contained within the memory sets of FS Parts. That means that a different Part of her provided her with the information she needed to share with the eight-year-olds as she age-progressed them.

I asked Mandy if she could identify the Part of her that provided her with the growing-up memories she shared with the three previously child Parts. She said, "Yes, I can feel the adult me who shared her memories. She has blond hair, with bangs, and her straight hair is shorter than mine. She's wearing a white gown and a green wreath on her head. Her primary job in my life seems to be recalling good times and building friendships. And yes, the children are now 20-year-old adults and they think sex with children is gross."

Neutralizing Secret Memories

I assume that all Parts were created in a time of need to protect the self (the Conscious Self; the patient). Even with Parts that insist their only function is to make the Conscious Self miserable, I assume that attitude was once, if not presently, helpful to the patient's survival. In this sense all Parts are or once were protectors of the whole person.

One type of protective Part is a "memory gatekeeper." This type of Part aims to prevent the patient (and the therapist) from knowing about some of the patient's disturbing memories, based upon its belief that the self is too weak to handle the pain. Sometimes the gatekeeper itself is stuck in time and unaware that the child is now grown up. When informed of this, the gatekeeper may relent and permit us to work with the hidden memories. In other cases, however, it may continue to block access. With adequate time and resources, we could probably convince the gatekeeper that sharing the hidden memories would benefit the patient, especially since our healing work is based upon neutralizing disturbing memories. Fortunately, we have a work-around for well-meaning but uncooperative gatekeepers when the time available for therapy is limited. We can neutralize the secret memories without either the patient (Conscious Self) or the therapist knowing their content.

Once I have the agreement of the gatekeeper, I clarify the roles of each participant in the intervention. As the therapist, my role is to negotiate the intervention and recite the neutralizing narrative—wind, water, fire, etc. The Conscious Self's (patient's) role is to relay my guidance to the gatekeeper and visualize the intervention (e.g., a waterfall or a fire). The gatekeeper's job is to guide the visualized intervention to the SIM Part trapped in its pain. The gatekeeper must also relay information to the Conscious Self for sharing with me when difficulties appear during the neutralizing process, including any problems in reaching a SUD score of zero.

Sometimes there is an additional Freestanding (FS) Part that relays information between the Conscious Self and the memory gatekeeper. Once the memories are neutralized the gatekeeper may or may not share the hidden memories' contents. I've had both kinds of responses.

Case Example: Neutralizing Secret Memories.
My patient was 13 years old and a student in the eighth grade. She was depressed and met diagnostic criteria for

dissociative identity disorder (DID). I will call her Sybil. I've also changed the name of the FS Part (i.e., the alter personality) with whom we worked. I will call her Sally. DID represents an extreme form of dissociative disorder, characterized by the ability of at least two of its Parts to take full executive control of the person's body. Additionally, the patient must be amnesic for whatever transpired during the time its Parts were in executive control.

I could have had direct conversations with Sally and exiled Sybil to the nonconscious world if Sally had taken full executive control from Sybil. However, my preference is to work with DID patients in the same way I work with non-DID patients. Consequently, I directed all of my work with Sally through Sybil with Sybil fully in executive control.

During the third month of our weekly meetings, we ran into the problem of hidden memories. We had already done some healing work with Sally, but she resisted further work because she didn't want either Sybil or me to know of certain memories that she insisted stay secret. She agreed to additional healing work when I explained that we could do the healing without her sharing her secrets with us. In this case, the FS Part and the memory gatekeeper were the same (Sally).

Sybil told me that Sally had examined her first secret memory and could visualize the SIM Part located in the scene. The SIM Part rated her disturbance at a level 7. We began the intervention, in which Sally brought the SIM Part to the waterfall visualized by Sybil, but after several minutes of silence, I asked what was happening. Sybil explained that Sally was stuck. The waterfall was not neutralizing the negative emotions. I coached Sybil to suggest that Sally look carefully around the memory scene for a mother or father introject or some other Part that might be blocking. She found an older teen Part about age 16 that acknowledged being the blocker. (Note that Parts can present themselves as older than the patient.)

Working through Sally, we offered the teen blocker the Two-Step intervention in which the first step would be to place the negative emotions into a container for the teen's assessment. The teen responded with a flat, "No!" When asked why, Sally quoted the teen as saying, "Because you [the therapist] don't deserve it." I didn't have an answer for that.

I suggested that Sybil ask Sally to question the teen Part about its own earliest painful memory; the teen shared it with Sally. We then offered to heal the teen's memory. Once we learned that the teen had accepted our offer, Sybil guided Sally in neutralizing the teen Part's emotional memory in the waterfall. Sally soon reported a SUD score of zero for the teen Part's memory. The teen Part then gave our team permission to heal the original SIM Part's memory.

We were free again to carry out the original waterfall intervention for Sally's hidden memory. Sybil once more guided Sally in neutralizing the SIM Part's negative emotions in the waterfall. The result was a reduction of the original level 7 to a level 3 or 4. I suggested that Sybil repeat the intervention and invite the teen Part to join the SIM Part in the water. (I've found that previous blockers can become helpful assistants if given the opportunity.)

That worked to bring the SUD score to zero for the original hidden memory.

With the intervention complete, I asked if the teen Part would like to reveal itself to the patient. I also asked if the Part had a name. The teen said it had a name but didn't want to reveal it or its image to Sybil. It wanted to remain "super-secret." Two weeks later, we used the same protocol with two of Sally's additional memories. We neutralized these two memories (dating to ages 5 and 6) to a SUD score of zero without interference from any other Parts.

Emotion, Not Fact, Disappears

Parts and Memory Therapy aims to neutralize the implicit emotional memories of disturbing events while affecting explicit factual, autobiographical memories as little as possible. After we replace pain or other negative emotions with neutrality, what is left is the factual narrative of a previously disturbing event. The facts, including the fact that the memory was once painful, remain. I often suggest that what remains is a narrative of events similar to a factual history book, enlightening perhaps but not emotional.

Sometimes, the focus is on the memory of a body sensation of physical pain that a Part continues to feel—such as one of my patient's sensations of pain connected to his years-before open-heart surgery. And sometimes the focus can be on physical pleasure, such as that associated with an addiction to pornography. It might even be on a child Part's conflicting physical stimulation when we neutralize the confusion and distress caused by inappropriate touching by an adult. We should neutralize both the negative and positive emotional memories in such cases. The factual narrative remains, however, and continues to serve as a source of wisdom for future action.

Earliest Memories for Healing Chronic Abuse

When working with a chronically traumatized patient, the earliest painful memory may be difficult to neutralize because of intrusions from later, similar memories. For example, as we strip negative emotions from the first memory, similar emotional distress from later memories may replace what we've just cleared from the first memory, leaving us with no gain. In such cases, I will guide the patient to construct mental barriers in the form of domes, walls, or force fields between the first memory and later memories. In this way we ideally prevent unwanted intrusions into the initial memory scene and avoid a chain reaction of distress in the internal system. Once we've neutralized the first memory in the chain, later memories heal more easily.

When Parts Disappear

Among the problems that can arise when working with a newfound Part is a tendency for it to disappear, especially when you're still getting acquainted. Usually, a newly emerged Part will return when asked. Your patient need only say something like, "Hey! Come back, please!"

In other cases, coaching your patient to ask for the Part's manager or boss can be helpful in bringing a hidden Part into view. If the Part has or says it has no boss, you've lost nothing. It's just a ploy that sometimes works and sometimes doesn't. But this request often brings a manager or boss into view. When the manager appears, you have the opportunity to negotiate for access to the hidden FS Part.

In still other cases, the FS Part you're looking for seems unable to show itself without help. The affect bridge is a useful tool here. You would ask the patient to focus on his current emotions or feelings while letting his mind float back to his earliest disturbing memories. Whatever the patient is feeling will be linked to the memories you elicit because at this point in time they occupy the same emotional universe. Thus, you can ask your patient to focus on his anger; whatever comes up will be connected to that anger.

Clinical Example.
A patient I will call Ben came to therapy to reduce his problem anger. At first, he was unable to generate an image of his angry Part. Nor could he think of an experience, situation, or person that produced an angry feeling. However, he had previously identified his father as a primary source of anger because of the childhood beatings his father gave him.

By focusing upon his feelings toward his father and then letting his mind float back to the earliest memory that came up, he could bridge to an experience from age four. His mother had asked him what he had done with her sewing needle. She said that she always left it in the same place—her sewing basket—but the needle was missing. Since only she and Ben were present in the house, he must have taken it. He repeatedly denied touching her needle but she didn't believe him.

When his father came home from work, he joined his mother to demand that Ben reveal what he did with the needle. Ben didn't know. So his father would beat him, demand to know what he did with the needle, then beat him some more. As the beatings continued, Ben tried to guess where the needle might be. But he never guessed correctly. Finally, his mother rechecked her sewing basket and found the needle underneath some other items. Neither parent apologized to Ben.

Ben successfully viewed himself in the third person as his four-year-old self (a SIM Part) and then as his five-year-old self (a second SIM Part), and in both cases neutralized the associated memories. But we still couldn't locate the angry FS Part. I asked Ben to speak to the child Parts he had located in the two memories and to ask them to take him to their boss, manager, or protector.

They responded that they were too afraid to do so. But when asked to point in the boss's direction, one of them gestured over its shoulder with its thumb to the woods behind the beach (we had used an ocean metaphor in washing away their disturbing emotions). Eventually, by projecting his voice into the woods, Ben convinced the angry Part to show itself and share additional disturbing memories.

Relieving Current-Time Stress

The "memory" in Parts and Memory Therapy should not be taken to mean that the model's effectiveness is limited in any way to old or new memories, although one difference is that with current events, FS and SIM Parts may appear to be identical. The same types of rituals we use to neutralize hurtful memories of the distant past work just as well to neutralize current-time stress and anxiety.

Examples are endless but include harassment by bosses and coworkers, overwhelming workloads, low pay, spousal indifference and anger, children's grades, and critical mothers-in-law. Any of these experiences that happen today quickly slide into the past of yesterday. So too does an anticipated stressful event for tomorrow almost instantly become a memory of an anticipated event that we can neutralize before it becomes today's event.

To a high degree, neutralizing an imagined future event serves to inoculate a patient with protection against the event ahead of its arrival. For example, by guiding the patient in your office to visualize getting fired you enable her to experience the same anxiety she experiences outside your office. And when you help her neutralize that visualized event, the neutrality she feels before leaving your office continues outside your office for shorter or longer periods of time, depending upon other variables.

The point is that we can just as easily neutralize current-time memories as we do memories from decades ago. For example, a patient I will call Thomas had been angry for three days before our session. A coworker had made a complaint about him to their boss. Thomas was angry in part because the complaint was unjustified, and also because he had helped the coworker get his job. Thomas felt both unfairly accused of wrongdoing and betrayed by a friend. At the time of our session, he was angry for his fourth consecutive day. He could visualize himself as the SIM Part in the memory scene from four days earlier when he learned of the betrayal.

He was a veteran at neutralizing memories because of our earlier work on his more distant past and quickly adapted his skills to deal with his recent memories. He accepted my guidance in pointing out to the angry SIM Part that its anger was not helping him (the Conscious Self) and that helping should be its primary role. The Part quickly accepted Thomas's request to retain the wisdom that came with experiencing the betrayal and allow Thomas to visualize a powerful wind blowing away the negative energy still attached to the memory. The intervention took no more than 30 seconds and followed 20 minutes of discussing the problem and its solution.

Returning Negative Emotions to Their Source

In some situations, we cannot easily release a Part's dysfunctional behaviors or beliefs through the standard set of neutralizing rituals. It may be that the emotions don't result from personal experience of trauma; instead, they may be downloaded from a parent. For example, a wife's lifetime of high anxiety about her husband's possible cheating or her belief that there are unseen and ubiquitous dangers in the world for which the patient must always be alert, might have passed these issues on to her child (the patient) through the child's identification with the mother. In such cases, a ritual in which you guide your patient to visualize the SIM Part returning its negative emotions to the parent may be appropriate.

Such a ritual might go something like this (speaking to your patient): "Ask the Part to locate where it feels the distress in its body and then visualize lifting it out of itself and handing it back to the mother who gave it to you." You might suggest that the patient speak to the mother (either as a mother introject or in whatever context she can find the mother's image) and say something like, "I know you've been trying to protect me with your concerns and you've helped me to grow up. Thank you. But I don't need these fears (or anger or sadness, etc.) anymore. I'm giving them back to you."

SIM Part as Target

As I pointed out earlier in the book, when neutralizing memories, it's most efficient to work directly with the SIM Part rather than the FS Part. The SIM Part continues to experience the trauma as it happened but the FS Part might view the event as relegated to the distant past with much less negative energy. When working first with the FS Part and neutralizing its SUD score for the memory, we might reach zero for this Part, but when we check with the SIM Part, we might discover that it retains a SUD level of 1 or 2. The SIM Part would require at least one more intervention to bring its SUD score to zero. However, when we work first with the SIM Part to achieve a zero SUD score, the FS Part almost always reaches a zero SUD score too.

SIM Parts in the Third Person.
Ideally, we want our patients to view the SIM Part of each memory from the third-person point of view, instead of our normal perception as we look out at the world from our own eyes with a first-person point of view. Interventions are much simpler when we can view our memory selves from outside of ourselves. Once the patient has the third-person view, we can immediately get the SIM Part's SUD score for the memory and then carry out the neutralizing intervention. (See pages 79-81, this chapter, for neutralizing SIM Parts still blended with the patient.)

In the first-person point of view, we see the memory scene through the eyes of the SIM Part just as we did when the events occurred. That makes it difficult to get an accurate SUD score from the SIM Part because it blends with the patient's assessment. But in the third person, not only do we get a good measure (for before-and-after comparison) of the seriousness of the original event, the SIM Part's direct estimate on the SUD scale ensures the memory's reactivation in the mid-brain where we want to make changes. This reactivation is necessary for carrying out memory reconsolidation.

We want to be able to work with the SIM Part as if it were a separate entity. One way to maximize this is, as I noted earlier in the book, to ask first if the FS Part (rather than the patient) can view the SIM Part in the third person.

Over the years I've noticed the curious result that if I first ask this question of the patient, he is more likely to say no than if I first ask the FS Part if it can see the SIM Part in the third person. Once the FS Part acknowledges it has a third person view of the SIM Part, the patient is much more likely to share that view.

But what about the case where the FS Part can view the SIM Part in the third person, but the patient cannot—he can only view the scene in the first person through the SIM Part's eyes? In a case like this, to carry out the neutralizing intervention, we would treat the FS Part as if it were the SIM Part, utilizing the FS Part's SUD score to guide us to neutrality for the memory.

Resistance to Neutralizing

Given their ability to be coconscious with the Conscious Self, Freestanding Parts are generally aware of the need for change. Consequently, they rarely object when it's time to neutralize the negative emotions and sensations attached to the multiple memories in their memory sets. When there is resistance, all that is usually required is for the patient to specifically request permission. My impression is that the FS Part just wants recognition of its own place in the process.

If the FS Part refuses permission, we must negotiate further with the Part. The Two-Step intervention described elsewhere (moving the negative emotions temporarily into a separate container for assessment) generally resolves the issue. If more is required, it's likely because a powerful system manager working behind the scenes is the hold-up. In that case we have to find the blocker and deal with its objections. In the paragraphs below, I summarize the most frequent reasons Parts object to our therapy. (I mentioned some of these issues in earlier chapters.)

1. Current Threats Block Healing of Earlier Trauma.
Sometimes a manager will object that we cannot neutralize the targeted memory because the same painful experiences continue in the present. Aside from working with the patient to remove herself from her current situation, I've found the most effective way to move forward is to isolate the targeted memory from later or everyday stresses with a visualized wall, barrier or dome that permits neutralizing without activating other memories. I noted previously that this technique permits neutralizing earlier memories separately from later memories in cases of chronic abuse.

2. The Belief that Disturbing Emotions Protect.
Parts may believe that the emotional memories that frame narrative memories are necessary for them to fulfill their functions, especially protecting the self or other vulnerable Parts. The opposite is more likely to be the case—that is, by holding on to negative energy associated with particular memories, a Part's ability to do its job diminishes.

A simple example would be the man who snaps at his wife when she asks for clarification of some matter. Later, he may apologize and suggest that his work had stressed him out. But some damage has been done and his behavior will likely repeat in the future, further damaging his relationship. Suppose we can bridge from his snappishness to experiences in which his father frequently mistreated him. The angry Part may initially insist that the man needs to continue to be angry with his father to protect himself from others who might injure him.

Unfortunately, when the negative energy in those life experiences makes the man snappish with his wife, the Part's negative emotions harm the self by creating a problematic relationship with his wife. When the angry Part accepts the neutralizing of his father's mistreatment, he may find that he's able to avoid snapping at his wife and instead find himself patient with his wife's queries.

3. Fear of Loss of an Emotional Guide.

As one patient observed after we had neutralized his guilt over not being more attentive and sensitive during the months before his mother died of cancer, "You dilute the lessons learned from experiences if you continue to carry around the baggage from the lesson." We had just neutralized the guilty Part who didn't at first believe he would remain sensitive to the needs of others if he released the final portion of his guilt. He had given up about 80% of it but insisted that he keep the remainder to remind him of his previous failure. Using a Two-Step intervention in which my patient helped the Part temporarily place the remaining negativity into a container before permanently neutralizing it, my patient was able to demonstrate to the Part that his ability to play its role was enhanced rather than diminished.

4. Fear of Becoming Weak.

Angry Parts often express their concern with becoming too weak to protect the patient if they neutralize their anger. In general, angry Parts are uncooperative when asked to neutralize particular memories. It can be helpful to work with a minor incident to demonstrate to the angry Part that its fears of becoming weak are unfounded.

In the case of a 52-year-old man whose anger pushed him farther and farther away from his jealous 60-year-old girlfriend, the angry Part agreed to allow a single demonstration that neutralizing a memory would not reduce its strength. The girlfriend was insecure in their relationship. She regularly accused her boyfriend of inappropriate relationships with other women, based upon little or no evidence. She would take the most innocent of interactions or comments and interpret them as indications that her boyfriend had an inappropriate interest in someone else.

There were so many of these incidents that I convinced the angry Part that healing just one of these memories would pose no threat. The incident was relatively minor; the girlfriend had accused the boyfriend of lustfully looking at their waitress at lunch. This sort of thing had happened many times. The neutralizing ritual produced a SUD score of zero for the memory in less than a minute (although negotiations for the demonstration took half an hour). Eventually, following additional, similar interventions, the angry

Part discovered that it hadn't become weak, and learned to be tolerant of his girlfriend's fears.

More on Working with Blockers

"Blocker" is a descriptive term that refers to a Part causing us difficulty in neutralizing memories. Over many years of sometimes-frustrating experiences, I've learned that when a difficulty arises in carrying out a neutralizing ritual, the source is usually a nearby blocking Part. This Part, perhaps for reasons unknown even to itself, interferes with the healing. When this happens you wisely recognize the problem and seek out the blocking Part rather than continue attempting to neutralize with more powerful imagery (e.g., going from a misty rain intervention to a powerful hurricane).

Blocking Parts can be most easily found by simply asking the patient to look around the memory scene while asking that the Part do the same, and check whether another Part is visible, perhaps on the periphery of the intervention scene. Inevitably, such an observer is the blocker.

Sometimes you can find the blocker—or communicate with it—by suggesting that your patient speak into the memory scene and advise the presumed hidden blocker that you are requesting permission to complete the intervention. It should say "yes" or "no"—and no answer means "yes." You may get a disembodied "yes," or "no" or the blocker may show itself, permitting direct negotiation. If no answer, then try the intervention again. You can probably carry it out now.

Blocking can be recognized when the visualized intervention fails to affect the SIM Part. For example, in a wind intervention, the wind may appear to go over or around without reaching the SIM Part, or when a rainfall intervention may not wet the Part while falling all around it. In a variation of this sort of block, you may guide your patient repeatedly in a neutralizing ritual, but the reduction in the SUD level decreases only incrementally (i.e., from a level 6 to a 5 to a 4 and then a vague, "Maybe a 3.5.)." Or, the SUD level of a given disturbing memory stubbornly remains at a 1 or 2.

Parts Don't Go Away Forever

Parts don't go away, except temporarily, or, on rare occasions, after they neutralize all negative emotions that previously distressed them. Even then, I suspect they are only dormant, and will reappear if the patient is challenged by new experiences similar to those they previously healed.

Frequently, the Conscious Self, blended with a strong manager, may want to rid himself of a problem Part, such as a raging Part that causes problems with his relationships. But such a Part is structurally a part of the whole personality system and we cannot remove it selectively from the system. In any case, it wouldn't be helpful to do so because rage is just the extreme pole of anger. Getting rid of anger entirely would leave a patient powerless in many situations. Being able to be angry is essential for human functioning, even if it's only mild anger.

Being appropriately angry allows us to protect ourselves from exploiters and gives us the energy to stand up for ourselves when we should. Rather than getting rid of extreme Parts, the goal of Parts and Memory Therapy is to help the patient guide the Part in neutralizing the painful life experiences that created its extreme way of being. In this way we bring the anger down to an appropriate level.

It's also important to recognize that a patient who wants to get rid of a Part is expressing the wish of another Part, seamlessly blended with the Conscious Self: a manager hoping to win out over a competing Part. In P&MT, we view any strong emotion, belief, or conviction expressed by a patient as best understood as the expression of a blended Part and having its own agenda. I would want to make this point to my patient. When feasible, I would also like my patient to become acquainted with this Part and to develop a cooperative relationship with it. The manager is an ally and perhaps the strongest motivation for a patient to come to therapy in the first place.

Case Example.
It's possible to visualize a Part killing or otherwise disposing of another Part. The patient might be temporarily freed from the offending Part, but only temporarily. In one of my cases, a Part named *The Judge* blocked almost all of our efforts to heal wounded child and juvenile Parts. One manager activated a Part called *The Hit Man*. Unguided by me, my patient visualized The Hit Man going up to the Judge and shooting him with a handgun multiple times. The Judge disappeared temporarily, but reap-

peared again within five days, still resisting the process of healing.

It might be possible to block a Part from interacting with other Parts for an even longer period of time. However, the apparently blocked Part would simply influence the patient nonconsciously and thus become even more challenging to work with. It's better to interact with an uncooperative Part in the clear.

Occasionally, a Part that has completed the neutralizing of all of its painful memories will have no interest in playing a new role in the system. Instead, the Part might indicate it was going on vacation or just going to relax on a beach indefinitely. In one case, a Part said to my patient that it would "tour the world." She watched internally as the Part walked away, waving goodbye.

Ending a Session

It's best to stop processing new traumatic material at least 10 minutes before the end of the session. Otherwise, you run into the danger of your patient leaving the office with only partially processed material. Depending upon the nature of the material accessed (but not processed), your patient may have a difficult time with those emotions during the next few days. If angry, your patient may get in more arguments with her husband; if sad, she may feel more depressed, etc. Better to wait until the next session to open up more painful memories for processing when there may be insufficient time to finish.

When your patient has activated painful memories but has not fully processed them by the end of the session, the best procedure is to help the Part involved place the activated negative emotions into a (metaphorical) container for processing during the following session. The container can be anything acceptable to the Part, a purse, a bottle, a safe or a Tupperware container. This temporary storage has the added benefit of demonstrating that the emotional memories can indeed be safely separated from the Part, making final neutralizing that much easier to achieve.

Another technique I've found helpful in such cases is to ask my patient to visualize the Part taking a week's vacation in a comfortable place, perhaps on a Hawaiian beach, a mountain meadow, a comfortable bed, or floating on a cloud. Sending a Part on a vacation is also helpful when working with substance addiction. Often, it will help your patient get through the difficult time of physical withdrawal while the addicted Part distances from conscious awareness.

Case Example.
Here's an example of a person leaving our work space with unresolved emotional memories (she was in a dissociative state). She was a therapist leaving our workshop following an experiential learning exercise. She had volunteered to be a practice patient for another therapist-in-training to learn the basic technique of finding a Part and neutralizing an embarrassing moment from elementary school.

As it turned out, we connected the embarrassing moment to a set of autobiographical memories of a five-year-old FS Part. A week later, she reported that the five-year-old Part had stayed with her for four days before ceasing to blend with her. She added that the dissociative blending was so powerful that as she drove home from the workshop, and for another three days, she could "feel" the five-year-old's "double pony tail" pulling at her own hair. She found herself reaching up to her hair to be sure it was down and not pulled into a double pony tail. She also said that when she looked into a mirror, she could "almost see" the five-year-old in the mirror in place of herself.

Further conversation with this therapist revealed that she had experienced chronic abuse in childhood. Our trainers had tried to screen for dissociative participants at the outset of the workshop, but our screening tool, the DES II, failed to register any significant dissociation.

Finding New Roles for Healed Parts

In bringing therapy to a successful close with grateful Parts, it's sometimes essential to help newly centered Parts to find a different job to do within the internal system. This adjustment isn't always necessary. SIM Parts are generally just happy to be freed from their painful memories. And most FS Parts aren't so narrowly locked into a role in the system as to require special attention. They may say they are going on vacation or intend to tour the world, but FS Parts with previously dominant roles (such as maintaining addictions, maintaining fear to protect against vulnerability, or raging at others to keep them at a distance) may feel empty unless they have new roles.

Some feel that having a job or role is necessary for their existence. These FS Parts may even refuse to cooperate with healing their own disturbing memories until the Conscious Self has found a new job for them. This attitude is understandable since they are in many ways alternate selves with years of investment in a patient's life. To deal with these Parts, I guide a negotiation between patient and Part for a new role that's mutually acceptable to both parties. Roles can be simple (e.g., take the time to smell the roses). or complex (e.g., monitor the ethical behavior of the patient).

Romantic Parts, healed of their attraction to inappropriate partners, may agree to help a patient with better decision-making in future dating. Panicky Parts may agree to make the patient aware of possible challenging situations without overwhelming him with anxiety. And frequently, a Part may accept a role that's roughly the opposite of its previous one. For example, a Part that had pressured the patient to avoid all social events might agree to encourage him to seek out social events that offered opportunities for career or social support. The nature of new roles is limited only by the imagination of the patient and Part. What's important is that a patient's Parts feel they positively contribute to the patient's life.

Chapter 7

Parts and Memory Therapy Protocols

I considered placing the contents of this chapter into an appendix following the primary text. But then I decided that although it consists predominately of tables, they are important enough to include in the text of the book, especially because the tables illustrate how the P&MT model can be helpful in working with virtually any issue or problem therapists are likely to face in the course of their careers.

Table 8. The Parts and Memory Therapy Protocol

The basic protocol for all P&MT work contains just four steps. They are easily stated, but much more complex when put into action.

1. DEFINE THE PROBLEM.
2. FIND THE PART THAT CARRIES THE PROBLEM.
3. ELICIT THE MEMORIES THAT ARE THE FOUNDATION FOR THE PROBLEM.
4. NEUTRALIZE THE PROBLEM MEMORIES.

Table 8, above, presents again the foundational protocol for Parts and Memory Therapy. It contains the orienting principles for work with the overwhelming majority of mental health problems. I placed it also at the beginning of Chapter 2 (Table 1), Chapter 3 (Table 2), Chapter 5 (Table 5), and Chapter 6 (Table 6). My intent is to remind therapists, as they work through the Guide, to keep in mind the broader framework of the model.

Additionally, I placed tables for three other protocols within the text of earlier chapters. The Step-Back protocol (Table 3) and the Twinning protocol (Table 4) appear in Chapter 4, "Parts Dynamics," representing calming or temporizing techniques, and both get heavy use. The Unmasking-Introjects Protocol (Table 7) appears in Chapter 6's intensive study of techniques for neutralizing emotional memories and for overcoming blocking Parts' efforts to block this work. Introjects may be the most frequent blockers of the neutralizing process.

The remaining 11 tables contain some of the protocols I've found especially useful over the last 15-20 years. This current compilation ranges from a multi-page protocol for training new therapists (Table 9) to a protocol for treating shy children as young as age 6 by utilizing a parent as surrogate for the child in telling the child's narrative of school refusal or other issues (Table 19).

The P&MT Training Protocol

When our trainers present Parts and Memory Therapy to a new class of professional therapists, we guide them through each step of the foundational protocol with explanations and illustrations of how the model works. Still to come are the experiential aspects of the training. For that, we divide the class into smaller groups of 4 to 6 trainees and ask each therapist to take a turn at the role of patient and therapist with one pair following the protocol and the other(s) as witnesses. The extended Training Protocol below guides them through the exercise and for reviewing the process.

Table 9. Parts and Memory Therapy Training Protocol
Define the Problem
1. Help your patient to be specific rather than abstract in defining the problem. For example, "I'm nervous in front of my boss," or "I'm too shy to speak in public." versus "I have low self-esteem."
2. Ask your patient to identify the emotion or body sensation connected to the problem.
Find the Part that Carries the Problem
3. Ask your patient to locate where in his body the emotion or sensation is strongest.
4. Ask your patient to speak to that emotion or feeling, silently or aloud, and ask it to give the patient an interactive image or picture of itself. When an image appears here or below, skip to item 9 below.
5. In the absence of an image in the patient's mind, ask the patient to speak to the emotion or feeling and request an increase (temporarily) of intensity of the sensation. A response means a Part is paying attention. Ask again for an image or a picture.

6. Ask your patient to direct the unseen Part to look into a mirror. What the Part sees, the patient will see.

7. If still no image, guide your patient in the "Two-Fishermen-With-a-Net" intervention.

8. If no image appears to the patient, treat the body sensation as you would an image and continue with the protocol. (Often, an internal image of the Part will show itself later in the process.)

9. Once your patient has located an image she can work with, verify with this FS Part that it's the one that claims as its own the issue you are treating.

10. Ask your patient to describe (for your notes) the FS Part she is visualizing: gender, hair color and style, clothes, age, and distinctive features you can use to find it in later sessions.

11. Spend some time just getting acquainted as you ask about its awareness of significant people in the patient's life—parents, siblings, children, spouse, etc.

Elicit the Memories that Are the Foundation for the Problem

12. Ask your patient to ask the FS Part to share its earliest disturbing memory of ANY kind. (Sometimes a patient or an FS Part will say a memory is not disturbing. If so, substitute other adverbs such as painful, distressing, bothersome, unpleasant, etc.)

13. Ask the patient to describe the memory in detail, especially what the patient's SIM Part is experiencing. (This will reactivate the emotional memory in the brain's relevant neural circuit.)

14. Ask the patient to ask the FS Part if it can see the memory's SIM Part in the third person, i.e., from outside itself. (Almost always the FS Part can do so.)

15. Ask the patient if she can see the SIM Part in the third person, i.e., from outside herself. (Asking the FS

Part and the patient, in that order, to view the SIM Part in the third person, increases the likelihood that the patient will have a third-person view. This permits the patient to interact directly with the visualized SIM Part without having to go through the FS Part.)

Neutralize the Problem Memories

16. Ask the SIM Part if it would like to let go of the negative emotions attached to the memory. (Note that a "no" answer to this question probably indicates the presence of a blocking Part. You may have to negotiate with the blocker before you can proceed.)

17. Rescue the SIM Part to a safe place. This provides escape from an intense trauma scene. It may also protect the SIM Part from interference by a nearby blocker. Skip this step if you can easily interact with the SIM Part embedded in the memory.

18. Carry out the neutralizing intervention with the SIM Part rather than the FS Part to be more efficient in reducing the SUD score to zero.

19. Make the FS Part your first target in neutralizing a memory only when the patient cannot visualize the SIM Part separately from himself (in the third person).

20. Ask the patient if she wants to use wind, water, fire or something else to release the SIM Part's distress. You may want to say, "We can blow it away with wind, wash it away with water, or burn it up in fire." You could also add, "Any visualization that symbolically erases the emotional energy will also work, including just throwing it away or flushing it down the toilet."

21. After the first pass of the intervention, ask the patient to check the SUD level for the Part. If the SUD level isn't zero, ask the Part if it knows why the SUD level isn't zero.

22. If the Part knows why the intervention is stalled, use that answer to focus the next pass of the intervention. If

the Part doesn't know why the intervention is stalled, simply repeat the intervention asking the Part to focus again on where in the body the memory is stored.

23. Continue repeating the intervention until the SUD level is zero. When the SUD level is a 1 or 2, visualizing - a big blast of hurricane wind will usually bring the SUD score to zero.

24. When there is significant resistance to neutralizing a memory, look for a blocking Part. Locate that Part and ask its permission to heal the Part of the pain of its memory.

25. To locate a blocking Part, ask the patient and the Part you're working with to "look around" to find the Part that might be observing the work. It could be a figure on the horizon, a parental introject, a shadow, a non-human image, or it might be hiding. Ask permission of the blocking Part (including a suspected unseen Part) to continue the intervention. Assert that only 3 responses are permitted: Yes, No, or no answer. No answer means Yes.

26. A blocking Part is often fearful of losing its power or disappearing. Reassuring the blocking Part that this isn't true is helpful in negotiating. Utilizing the "Two-Step" intervention usually seals the deal. (The Two-Step: Move the emotional energy first from the SIM Part into a container; check with the blocker to ascertain that nothing bad happened as a result of the transfer; neutralize the contents of the container.)

27. Return to the FS Part and elicit another memory for neutralizing.

The Shortcut Protocol

It's possible to utilize a truncated P&MT protocol without involving FS Parts when the patient just wants to heal a troubling one-off traumatic experience quickly. Sometimes other therapists will refer a patient to you for "trauma therapy" of a single experience but they wish to retain the patient for further treatment after you neutralize the problem. In these situations, you can be more efficient if you skip Step 2, finding the FS Part, and go directly from Step 1, defining the problem, to Step 3, eliciting the memories that are the foundation for the problem, where you can work directly with the SIM Part.

The shortcut is also a means of continuing your work when you've exhausted your toolbox of techniques for locating the FS Part that carries the problem but haven't managed to find it. The shortcut permits you to continue the therapy with the expectation that the FS Part will eventually show itself. Until then, you can focus upon direct work with the SIM Parts you locate through other means.

When we use the full 4-Step protocol, the FS Part located in Step 2 would ideally help us to find all of its linked or themed memories relevant to the original problem. We would elicit its earliest disturbing memory, neutralize it, go to the next memory, neutralize it also, and continue repeating the procedure until there are no other memories in that Part's memory set that require neutralizing.

When we take the shortcut, we can locate the memories in Step 3 of the protocol with an affect bridge (J. Watkins, 1971) or a Somatic Bridge (J. Watkins, 1992). To do this we ask the patient to focus on his emotion or body sensation and then let his mind go back in time to his first memory of experiencing the kind of emotion or body sensation he experiences at the moment. We would then neutralize the memory he locates by guiding him in work with the SIM Part embedded in the memory. We could continue to work with the additional memories his bridges call to our attention until his feelings change, disappear, or he runs out of memories.

The problem is that there may be other themed memories that make up the FS Part's memory set of which the patient is currently unaware. The Conscious Self (i.e., the patient) has no memories that are exclusively his own. All of his memories are stored in the memory sets of his FS Parts. If we cannot interact with his FS Part, the original issue (Step 1) may not be fixed because we don't have access to all relevant memories. Consequently, we would have to continue to search for the FS Part and its bundle of related memories.

Unlike the case when we work with the limited consciousness of a SIM Part, when we can work with the FS Part that caries the memories, we can dialog and explore questions of whether other memories are still available to us. Additionally, we can learn about the structure of the larger organization of Parts of the self. We can also develop the sorts of relationships with other FS Parts that contribute to pervasive healing. We should use the shortcut sparingly.

Table 10. The Shortcut Protocol
Define the Problem
1. Help your patient to be concrete rather than abstract in defining the problem. For example, "I'm nervous in front of my boss," or, "I'm too shy for public speaking" versus "I have low self-esteem," or, "My life is without purpose."

2. Ask your patient to identify the emotion or body sensation connected to the problem.

Elicit the Memories That Are the Foundation for the Problem

3. Use an affect or somatic bridge to elicit the memories that are the foundation for the problem. That is, guide the patient to focus on her emotion or body sensation and then let herself drift back in time to the earliest disturbing memory of any kind that comes up.

4. Guide your patient to locate and introduce herself to the SIM Part, visualized in the third person, and then to ask the Part to rate how disturbing its experience is on a 0-10 scale.

5. Ask the patient to describe the memory in detail, including the SIM Part's hair style and color, facial hair, and clothing. (This should be enough to reactivate the emotional memory in its memory circuit.)

Neutralize the Problem Memories

6. Ask the patient to ask the SIM Part if it would like to let go of the negative emotions attached to the memory. (Note that a "no" answer to this question indicates the presence of a blocking Part. You may have to negotiate with the blocker before you can proceed.)

7. Suggest that the patient rescue the SIM Part to a safe place if the memory scene is too distracting or intense for the intervention. This provides an escape from a painful trauma scene. It may also protect the no-saying SIM Part from interference by a nearby blocker.

8. Ask the patient if she wants to use wind, water, fire or something else to release the Part's distress. You may want to say, "We can blow it away with wind, wash it away with water, or burn it up in fire." You could also add, "Any visualization that symbolically dispenses with the emotional energy will also work, including just throwing it away or flushing it down the toilet."

9. Carry out the neutralizing intervention with the SIM Part.
10. After the first pass of the intervention, ask the patient to check the SUD level for the Part and, if the SUD level isn't zero, to ask if the Part knows why it isn't.
11. If the SIM Part knows why the intervention is stalled, use that answer to focus the next pass of the intervention. If the Part doesn't know why the intervention is stalled, repeat the intervention with a more powerful metaphor. Feel free to suggest to the patient emotion words that might explain the stall.
12. Continue repeating the intervention until the SUD level is zero. When the SUD level is at 1 or 2, visualizing a big blast of hurricane wind or a powerful wave will usually bring the final SUD to zero.
13. When there is significant resistance to neutralizing a memory, look for a blocking Part. Locate that Part and ask its permission to heal the Part of the pain of its memory.
14. To locate a blocking Part, ask the patient and the Part you're with to "look around" to find the Part that might be observing the work. It could be a figure on the horizon, a parental introject, a shadow, or a non-human image. Ask permission of the blocking Part to continue the intervention. When there is an unresponsive blocking Part, say to this Part that no response means "yes, permission given."
15. A blocking Part is often fearful of losing its power or disappearing. Reassuring the blocking Part that this isn't true is helpful in negotiating. Suggesting the "Two-Step" intervention usually seals the deal. (The Two-Step: Move the emotional energy from the SIM Part into a container; check with the blocker to see that what it feared would happen, didn't; neutralize the contents of the container.)
16. Return to the body sensation or emotion and elicit another memory for neutralizing.

The Hotspot Trauma Protocol

The Hotspot Protocol utilizes a 3-part (normal, traumatized, new normal life) narrative of a portion of a patient's autobiography in order to place the targeted trauma(s) in a larger context of life experience. It's especially useful when traumatic events are chronic or when lesser disturbing events occur over a period of time before peaking as a major trauma or high-energy distressing event or condition. One example is postpartum depression where a woman experiences a difficult pregnancy and childbirth culminating eventually with an extensive amount of time in a postpartum depressed state. As we elicit the narrative we would note (perhaps with asterisks) the hotspots of disturbing experiences as they occurred in both the lead-up to the targeted event, during the event(s), and afterwards when our patients make painful adjustments to the new normal of everyday life (which may seem like it isn't "normal" at all).

The 3-part narrative links the trauma narrative to before and after versions of everyday life in order to reduce the traumatic impact on the patient's perception of the trauma as a singular and incomparable event in his personal life story. Life, death, joy and pain are normal events in all our lives. The bottom line is that we want to flatten the curve of the traumatic experiences so that after therapy, the patient will perceive the most extreme hotspot of emotional pain as more of a bump than a peak of distress.

Table 11. The Hotspot Trauma Protocol
1. Elicit the narrative of everyday life before and leading

up to the trauma. Note any high intensity moments within this narrative.
2. Elicit the narrative of the trauma, with special attention to the moments of high-energy hotspots; i.e., moments when the patient evinces a high score on the zero-10 SUD ("Subjective Units of Disturbance") scale. Note also your intuitive sense of a likely hotspot even if the patient fails to emphasize it.
3. Elicit the recovery narrative; i.e., how the patient got from the trauma to the new normal of current-time functioning (which might not be "normal" at all). Note any likely hotspots in this post traumatic adjustment.
4. Return to the hotspot narrative and systematically neutralize in historical order each hotspot through memory reconsolidation work with the Stuck-in-the-Memory Parts still mired in the negative emotions of the hotspots.
5. Before neutralizing a given hotspot, elicit a SUD score from the Stuck-in-the-Memory Part. This score will generally be higher than that elicited directly from the patient, unless it's already at the maximum of 10. Eliciting of the SUD score is essential for the coming memory reconsolidation because it assures that the memory is reactivated and available for editing.
6. Test the efficacy and completion of the trauma work by again eliciting the before, during, and after narrative. There should be no remaining hotspots.

Letting Go of Love

Letting go of love is an intervention useful for several psychotherapeutic situations. One situation perfect for this intervention is for the rejected partner in a couple breakup, where there is no hope of reconciliation. It would also be applicable when one partner in a couple is having an affair and wants to stop but the pull of the affair partner is too strong to release without help. Another is when a member of a couple is unable to fully commit to the couple relationship because of a lost love from the past, either recently or remotely (e.g., from middle school or high school age).

Table 12. Letting Go of Love Protocol
Note: Each step assumes that the therapist will talk to Parts through the Conscious Self (the patient). For this reason, I do not repeat "Ask the patient to ask the Part...."
1. Locate the romantic Part by asking the patient to recall a time when she was deeply in love and request that she speak to that emotion of love and request an image of it in her mind.
2. Guide the patient to introduce herself to this romantic Part and explain that she (the patient) is its future and that she needs the Part's help. Exchange enough information so that the Part and the patient have a good grasp of the current problem.
3. Request the FS romantic Part to give up its love for the problem ex "for the good of the team" (i.e., the whole person).
4. If the romantic Part agrees, carry out a standard neutralizing intervention with the focus on the Part's love rather than a negative emotion, using the SUE scale rather than the SUD scale.
5. If the romantic Part refuses, temporarily drop the request and ask the romantic Part for its earliest significant memory involving a love relationship. The romantic Part you find could be a SIM Part or a different, intrusive FS Part in love with a different ex. In either case, neutralize the Part's love. Then check again to see if the first romantic Part is now ready to let go of its problematic love.

If so, neutralize that love.
6. If the first romantic Part continues to resist neutralizing, go to as many other previous love relationships as needed and neutralize them, continuing until the original romantic Part is flexible enough to neutralize its problem love. If necessary, go back even to the "childhood crush on the fourth-grade boy in the second row, third seat."
7. Sometimes, you may have to neutralize the painful memories of breaking up, but if you can neutralize love first, the painful aspects of the relationships will dissipate on their own.

Trichotillomania, Excoriation, Nail Biting

Trichotillomania (hair-pulling), excoriation (skin-picking), and onychophagia (nail-biting) are classified in the DSM 5 in the section of Obsessive-Compulsive and Related Disorders (American Psychiatric Association, 2013). I've had good success with neutralizing nail-biting and trichotillomania, and I've found that when we neutralize trichotillomania, the effects apply to a patient's skin-picking as well. I suspect that any of the repetitive disorders listed with the obsessive-compulsive disorders would respond well to the protocol below.

The protocol begins with asking the patient to prepare to pull hair, pick skin, or bite a fingernail (or cuticle) but stop the action before actually doing so. The unfinished action produces a discomfort and an urge to complete the action. This discomfort or urge connects us to the FS Part that carries the compulsion. We can then elicit the Part's disturbing memories (from earliest to latest) that must be neutralized for us to bring remission to the patient.

Table 13. Protocol for Trichotillomania, Excoriation, Nail Biting
1. Ask the patient to gently grasp a hair/eye-lash, prepare to pick a skin imperfection, or prepare to bite a nail, without following through on the action.
2. Ask the patient to focus on her urge to follow through on the action and then to request that the FS Part with that urge show her an image of itself. Introduce herself.
3. Guide the patient in developing rapport with the FS Part (e.g., Do they have the same views toward family members?). Then elicit the Part's earliest disturbing memory. (If unable to locate the FS Part, use an affect bridge to connect to an early memory).
4. Guide the patient to locate a third-person view of the Stuck-in-Memory (SIM) Part embedded in the memory. Explain herself and establish that the SIM Part wants help. (If unable to acquire a third-person view, substitute the FS Part for the SIM Part).
5. Elicit the SIM Part's SUD (0-10) score for the distress it feels as it experiences the remembered events.
6. Neutralize the SIM Part's disturbing emotion(s) with imagined wind, water, fire, or other symbolic cleansing actions until the Part's SUD score is zero for the memory.
7. Return to the FS Part and repeat with a different memory and SIM Part.
8. Repeat earlier steps as needed. Follow the same process at the next session.

P&MT Protocol for Treatment of Addictions

In this short introduction I will speak about all addictions without making a distinction as to whether the addiction causes permanent changes in the brain—or even temporary changes--nor will I make a distinction between those which are most harmful to the person or may lead to long-term damage.

The vast majority of addictions seem to be treatable through a single protocol, with some adjustments made to accommodate special cases that some types of addictions may bring. Addictions I have treated over the last 25 years include alcohol and drugs, smoking, pornography, shoplifting, and gambling, I have worked the least with alcohol and drugs and have found that for me personally these are the most difficult to work with because of the difficulty of keeping such patients in therapy. They have so many distractions that can cause them to leave therapy for shorter or longer periods until they recognize again the self-defeating nature of such avoidances. I've been most successful with porn and gambling addictions. Regardless of my own degree of success with these addicts, I strongly believe that the protocol works for all of them under the right conditions (uninterrupted weekly or bi-weekly sessions without major setbacks of returning to the addiction prior to the completion of the therapy).

I first developed a treatment protocol for porn addiction and eventually found that the same protocol was suitable for all of the addictions I had seen. Of course, some adjustments must be made for the content of the addiction, but the framework for treatment is applicable to all of my group of addicts.

What they all have in common is painful trauma or trauma-like experiences, or major attachment losses in their lives across their lifespans, especially during the elementary school years. Second, each of them, in addition to their addiction, derives a significant level of pleasure from engaging in the addiction type.

Table 14. Protocol for Treatment of Addictions
1. Identify the type of addiction.
2. Find the addicted Part by asking the patient to imagine engaging in the addiction activity and activate the feeling of pleasure or relief that accompanies that visualization.
3. For example, a smoker might visualize himself taking his first cigarette inhale of a new day; a drug or alcohol user might locate the sensation that comes with the first wave of intoxication; a porn addict could think about his favorite pornographic image and feel the first sensations of arousal.
4. Guide the patient to speak to the addictive response he has located and request that the Part that provides the response to "Please give me a picture or image of you in my mind." When there is no response, use techniques such as asking the Part to look into a mirror or use the Two-Fishermen-with-a-Net tool (Chapter 3) to locate the Part.
5. Develop rapport with the addicted Part by asking how old it is, whether it knows the patient is married, whether the patient's spouse or partner is also its spouse or partner, whether it knows the patient's occupation, etc. (Note: sometimes an addicted Part will have no memo-

ries or knowledge of the patient's everyday life except when the patient is engaging in his addiction.)
6. Elicit the Part's earliest disturbing memory of any kind and neutralize it. (Note: the memories don't have to be about the addiction.)
7. Use the affect bridge (Chapter 6) to find relevant early memories when you are unable to find an image of the addicted Part.
8. Continue eliciting and neutralizing the addicted Part's memories from the earliest to the present time.
9. Doing the neutralizing work should make the addicted Part and the patient flexible enough that they agree to neutralize the positive emotional memories that derive from the addiction. Neutralize those positive experiences from the earliest to the most recent memories.
10. When you have neutralized the addiction by neutralizing both of the addicted Part's chains of negative and positive memories, find a way to integrate the previously addicted Part into the patient's everyday life. For example, invite the previous porn addict to join the patient's non-porn sex life; e.g., suggest that the addicted Part be a lookout for tempting contexts to avoid.

Treatment of IBS and Fibromyalgia

The following protocol is based upon recent experiences treating irritable bowel syndrome (IBS) but it applies also to fibromyalgia and any other chronic pain condition where there is no clear physiological explanation for the pain or distress. I have been fortunate in bringing both IBS and fibromyalgia to remission. However, sometimes patients experience improvements in their conditions but do not reach complete remission.

Table 15. Protocol for Treatment of IBS, Fibromyalgia

1. Ask the patient to focus on the pain/distress she feels (including body pain, diarrhea, cramping, nausea) and to speak to the sensation, asking it to give her an image of itself.

2. When unable to locate the FS Part, use an affect bridge to connect to an early memory and go to step 6.

3. Guide the patient to establish rapport with the FS Part ensuring that the Part knows it's a Part of the patient. Ask whether it knows the patient's age, family members, and claims them as its own. Explain that the patient has come to help the Part reduce its pain or distress.

4. Ask the Part to share its earliest disturbing memory of any kind.

5. If the Part cannot settle on a particular memory as its earliest, substitute a request for any early disturbing memory.

6. Neutralize the distress of the SIM Part embedded in the memories, utilizing wind, water, fire, or another symbolically powerful force.

7. When the SUD score doesn't easily reach zero, repeat the neutralizing intervention with increased strength in the imagery or choose a different intervention.

8. When unable to reach a SUD score of zero, assume there is intrusive energy from a Part's earlier memory or a current-time blocking manager. If there is an earlier memory, neutralize that memory first. If the blocker is an FS manager Part, negotiate for permission to neutralize the targeted memory, with lots of praise for the Part's wisdom and strength.

9. When no image of the blocking Part appears, speak to the entire memory scene, including its horizons, and

again request permission. Assert the double-bind rule that only 3 answers are possible: YES, NO, or NO ANSWER, and NO ANSWER means YES, permission granted.
10. Following steps 8 or 9, carry out the neutralizing intervention.
11. During later sessions, repeat the process of locating and neutralizing disturbing memories linked to pain or other distressing symptoms until the symptoms disappear.

Protocol for Treatment of PMS/PMDD

Premenstrual dysphoric disorder (PMDD) represents the extreme form of premenstrual syndrome (PMS). The DSM 5 now recognizes PMDD as a legitimate diagnosis and places it among the depressive disorders. As shown by Table 16, symptoms are not limited to depression. To meet criteria for diagnosis the patient must experience at least 5 symptoms. At least 1 symptom must match a symptom from the first 4 sets listed. Criteria must be met for 3 consecutive months and the patient must experience "clinically significant distress or interference with work, school, usual social activities, or relationships with others" (American Psychiatric Association, 2013).

Table 16. Premenstrual Dysphoric Disorder Symptoms
1 Mood swings, sudden sadness, crying or increased sensitivity to rejection
2 Irritated, angry, or increased conflict

3 Hopeless, depressed, or putting yourself down
4 Anxious, tense, or on edge
5 Decreased interest in usual activities
6 Difficulty concentrating
7 Lethargic, lack of energy
8 Appetite change, craving certain foods, or overeating
9 Insomnia or hypersomnia
10 Overwhelmed or feeling out of control
11 Physical symptoms, like joint or muscle pain, tender or swollen breasts or feeling bloated

PMDD has shown itself to be a difficult condition to treat. The most popular treatments are based upon either serotonin reuptake inhibitors (SSRIs) or Cognitive Behavioral Therapy (CBT). Meta-studies of these approaches, however, have failed to show significant benefits for PMDD patients (Hallbreich, U., 2008; Kleinstauber, et al., 2012; Lustyk, et al.,2009).

In contrast to these reports, I've found rapid benefits for PMDD sufferers using Parts and Memory Therapy. In 10 case studies of PMDD treatment utilizing this approach, 9 out of 10 achieved complete remission of PMDD; that is, they no longer met criteria for PMDD.

Table 17. PMS/PMDD 22 Symptom Ratings

Cognitive/Emotional	Circle One	Physiological	Circle One
Angry/Irritable	0 1 2 3 4	Dizzy/Fainting	0 1 2 3 4
Anxious	0 1 2 3 4	Fatigue	0 1 2 3 4
Mood swings	0 1 2 3 4	Food Cravings	0 1 2 3 4
Nervous tension	0 1 2 3 4	Headache	0 1 2 3 4
Overwhelmed	0 1 2 3 4	Palpitations	0 1 2 3 4
Suspicious	0 1 2 3 4		

Cognitive/Emotional	Circle One	Physiological	Circle One
Confused	0 1 2 3 4	Abdominal bloating	0 1 2 3 4
Crying	0 1 2 3 4	Breast tenderness	0 1 2 3 4
Depressed	0 1 2 3 4	Cramping	0 1 2 3 4
Forgetful	0 1 2 3 4	Swollen hands/feet	0 1 2 3 4
Insomnia/Hypersomnia	0 1 2 3 4	Weight gain	0 1 2 3 4
Less interest usual activities	0 1 2 3 4		

Add total Score: _____

After 5 sessions, the 10th patient reduced her PMDD symptoms by about 30 percent but still met PMDD diagnostic criteria. Two months after our 5th session, she commented, "My PMDD is definitely not in remission although my symptoms are not as severe nor do they seem to last as long. My anger is less and my sadness is the same. My strategies for coping work quite well now when I actively remember and choose to use them."

Most PMDD patients respond quickly and many are close to remission after only three to five sessions of P&MT treatment. Note that treatment should take place during the PMDD phase of a woman's cycle. At other times of the month, the Freestanding Parts that drive the symptoms may not be reachable.

Table 18. Protocol for P&MT Treatment of PMS/PMDD
1. Meet with your patient on a day when she is actively experiencing PMDD symptoms. Schedule future sessions on symptomatic days also.
2. Patient should complete the 22-item, PMS/PMDD symptom questionnaire.
3. Patient should choose a currently disturbing PMDD symptom from her ratings on the 22-item questionnaire.
4. Find the Freestanding (FS) Part by asking the patient to focus on the symptomatic emotion or body sensation and speak to it, aloud or silently, and ask it to give her an image of itself as it views itself; or look into a mirror and the image will appear also in the patient's mind; or use the Two-Fishermen-with-a-Net technique (Chapter 3) to locate the reluctant Part.

5. If unable to locate the FS Part, guide the patient in using an affect bridge (Chapter 6) to find an early disturbing memory and find its Stuck-in-the-Memory (SIM) Part. Then go to item 11.

6. Note for later recall the FS Part's age, color and style of clothing and hair, etc.

7. Develop rapport with the Part by asking questions about shared views of family and friends.

8. Ask the FS Part to share its earliest disturbing memory of any kind.

9. Patient should ask the FS Part if it can visualize the memory's SIM Part in the third person. Then ask the patient if she can also view the SIM Part in the third person. (Doing this in this order increases the probability of a third-person view for the patient.)

10. When the patient cannot achieve a third-person view of the SIM Part, substitute the FS Part for the SIM Part as the target for the neutralizing intervention.

11. Guide the patient in using wind, water, fire, toilet flush, or some other symbolically powerful action to neutralize the SIM Part's disturbing emotions or body sensations.

12. Repeat the process by returning to the FS Part and elicit its next disturbing memory.

13. When the FS Part no longer has disturbing memories, guide the patient in picking another PMDD symptom and repeat the protocol.

14. Repeat the protocol the next day if PMDD symptoms persist. Otherwise, repeat the protocol during the next PMDD phase of the patient's cycle in the following month. Expect some regression of symptoms' SUD scores for the next month.

Protocol for Treatment of Shy Children

A special problem arises when the patient is too shy to talk in front of the therapist, but has no problem talking with her parent elsewhere. In such cases, a possible workaround involves guiding a parent as the child's surrogate in playing the role of the child during interaction with the therapist. I've been successful in treating two such patients.

The first was a 5-year-old girl in my office with her mother; the second was a 9-year-old girl in my office with her father. Both children experienced significant nausea and stomach pain on school days, with the 5-year-old actually vomiting before school. In both cases the children overcame their involuntary physiological responses by closely monitoring their parent as the parent pretended to be the child and followed the P&MT protocol. The underlying psychological issues for both children were attachment losses and fears of separation from their parents at school.

Case Example. Neutralizing School Refusal at Age 5.
The example is that of the 5-year-old mentioned above. The child's symptoms before each morning's departure for kindergarten were not her first episodes of pain and vomiting. The symptoms first arose at age 1.5 when her mother returned to work and left her daughter with her first nanny. They appeared again over the next 4 years with each change of nanny or preschool teacher, at ages 1.5, 3.5, 4.0, 4.5, 5.0 and 5.5. The child found immediate relief from vomiting and stomach pain when, following the protocol below in Table 19, her mother acted as her surrogate and role-played her in neutralizing her attachment losses.

Table 19. Utilizing a Surrogate for a Silent Child

1. Elicit a description and history of the problem from the parent as the child listens. Encourage the child to add or correct the parent's description—with whispers if needed. Note hotspots in parent's narrative for later neutralizing.

2. Guide the parent in role-play of the child, frequently addressing the parent by the child's name. The parent and child don't have to be of the same gender.

3. Child's role is to simply listen (but he/she is permitted to correct the parent at any time).

4. Repeat back to the parent-as-child the narrative previously elicited but stop at each emotional hotspot to carry out a neutralizing intervention of each problem memory; e.g., guide the parent-as-child to feel the waterfall you describe as it flows over, around and through her/him and washes away the child's painful emotional memories.

5. Parent-as-child accepts and affirms her internal changes as therapist's narrative and neutralizing interventions continue.

6. Neutralize each hotspot in chronological order, from earliest to most recent problem memory.

There are many more protocols that I could have included here, but this is a good sample. Careful examination and comparison of protocols will reveal that there is a great deal of repetition in the protocols. That follows from the nature of the 4-step foundational protocol around which the entire model is constructed. I encourage therapists who find this book valuable to construct their own protocols and share with other therapists.

References

American Psychiatric Association (2013). *Diagnostic and statistical manual of mental disorders (5th edition).* Arlington, VA: American Psychiatric Association.

Assagioli, R. (1965). *Psychosynthesis: A manual of principles and techniques.* New York, NY: Penguin Books.

Duvarci, S., & Nader, K. (2004). Characterization of fear reconsolidation. *The journal of neuroscience* 9269-9265

Ecker, B. (2018). Clinical translation of memory reconsolidation research: Therapeutic methodology for transformational change by erasing implicit emotional learnings driving symptom production. *International journal of neuropsychotherapy* 6: 1-92.

Ecker, B. & Brides, S. (2020). How the science of memory reconsolidation advances the effectiveness and unification of psychotherapy. *Clinical social work journal* 48: 287-300.

Ecker, B., Ticic, R., & Hulley, L. (2012). *Unlocking the emotional brain: Eliminating memories at their roots using memory reconsolidation.* New York: Rutledge.

Ecker, B., Ticic, R., Hulley, L. (2015). A primer on memory reconsolidation and its psychotherapeutic use as a core process of profound change. In Dahlitz, M. & Hall, G., Eds. *Memory reconsolidation in psychotherapy. The neuropsychotherapist special issue.* Park Ridge, Qld, Australia: The Neuropsychotherapist.

Hallbreich, U. (2008). Selective serotonin reuptake inhibitors and initial oral contraceptives for the treatment of PMDD: Effective but not enough. *CNS Spectrum* 13, 7, 566-572.

Kleinstauber, M., Witthoft, M., & Hiller, W. (2012). Cognitive-behavioral and pharmacological interventions for premenstrual syndrome or premenstrual dysphoric disorder: A meta-analysis. *Journal of clinical psychology in medical settings* 19(3), 308-319.

Kluft, R.P. & Fine, C., Eds. (1993). *Clinical perspectives on multiple personality disorder.* Washington, D.C.: American Psychiatric Press.

Lustyk, MKB., Gerrish, WG., Shaver, S., & Keys, SL. (2009). Cognitive-behavioral therapy for premenstrual syndrome and premenstrual dysphoric disorder: a systematic review: *Archives of women's health,* 12, 85.

Noricks, J. (1987). Testing for cognitive validity: Componential analysis and the question of extensions. *American Anthropologist* 89: 424-438.

Noricks, J. (2005). The psychology of Parts. Keynote address at the 13th annual conference, April 14-15, 2005. *Treating traumatic stress and dissociative disorders,* Morgantown, West Virginia: The Trauma Recovery Institute and West Virginia University School of Medicine, Department of Behavioral Medicine and Psychiatry.

Noricks, J. (2011). *Parts psychology: A trauma-based, self-state therapy for emotional healing.* Los Angeles: New University Press LLC.

Noricks, J. (2014). *For women only, book 1: Healing childbirth PTSD and postpartum depression with parts psychology.* Los Angeles: New University Press LLC.

Noricks, J. (2018). *Healing Amelia: Taming your ego states and inner voices with parts and memory therapy.* Los Angeles: New University press LLC.

Noricks J. (2020). How parts and memory therapy with memory reconsolidation bring remission to premenstrual dysphoric disorder (PMDD*). The science of psychotherapy*, February, 2020, 24-41. Park Ridge, QLD, Australia.

Rowan, J. (1990). *Subpersonalities: The people inside Us.* London: Rutledge.

Schreiber, F. R. (1973). *Sybil.* New York: Warner Books Inc.

Schwartz, R. C. (1995). *Internal family systems therapy.* New York: Guilford Press.

Watkins, H. H. (1980). The silent abreaction. *International Journal of clinical and experimental hypnosis,* XXVIII, 101-113.

Watkins, J. (1971). The affect bridge: A hypnoanalytic technique. *International journal of clinical and experimental hypnosis,* 19, 21-27.

Watkins, J. (1992). Psychoanalyse, hypnoanalyse, ego state therapie: Auf de Suche nach einer efffektiven Therapie: *Hypnose und Kognition, Band* 9,85-97.

Watkins, J. & Watkins, H. H. (1997). *Ego states: Theory and therapy.* New York: W.W. Norton.

Wolpe, J. (1969). *The practice of behavior therapy.* New York: Pergamon Press.

Glossary

AUDITORIUM: The imaginary safe place created during the Step-Back Technique, which the therapist coaches the patient to visualize. The stage, under the lights, is always occupied by the Conscious Self. The rows of seats ranging from 1 through 51, offer a safe degree of distance between the Conscious Self and Parts that might otherwise overwhelm and blend with the Conscious Self. The more powerful the Part, the further back. it should sit.

BLOCK: Used as a verb, this term refers to the action of interfering with some aspect of therapy.

BLOCKER: This is a descriptive term used to refer to any Part that interferes or seeks to interfere with the therapy.

CONSCIOUS SELF: This word refers to what most people mean when they use the term, "self." Self, thought of as singular by most people, is actually an agglomeration of Parts, smoothly linked together into a seamless entity. When we speak to others, we and they all experience the speech as coming from that singular self, but P&MT therapists view that communication as coming from the dominant Part of the self, influenced by others in a family of Parts with an interest or position in the topic of conversation. This group, including the speaker, constitutes the Conscious Self at that moment.

FREESTANDING PART: This the first of two primary types of Parts. A Freestanding or FS Part has been emancipated from any single memory to host its own unique set of themed memories. It isn't merely a self-representation of a single high-energy moment, such as when your parent died or when you first viewed your first-born child. An FS Part has a set of memories that has shaped its personality and function. It is coconscious with the Conscious Self or is capable of being so. The FS Part contains within its set of memories a total that ranges from a small number up to a number that charts the lifetime of the patient. When the patient talks about memories, she draws upon the memory sets carried by those Parts that are present at a given moment. She has no memories that are uniquely hers, but has access to all the memories of her FS Parts, except for a few that are intentionally kept from her by well-meaning managers.

FS PART: See Freestanding Part.

HOTSPOT: A traumatic or trauma-like hotspot experience is one that stands out from other experiences because of its greater disturbing energy in an autobiographical narrative.

IBS: Irritable bowel syndrome.

INSCAPE: This is the largely nonconscious world of Parts of the self. It refers to Parts' organization and structure and their relationships with each other. Generally, patients have little knowledge of their own inscapes. The term is synonymous with "inner world."

INTROJECT: In Parts and Memory Therapy, introjects are creations unconsciously created by patients, usually during their childhood and school years. They take the form of parents and other influential people who had a powerful impact on the development of the patient. Most introjects generally get in the way of our work by blocking our efforts to do therapy. If we cannot convince them to work with us, we have to unmask them. See Unmasking.

MANAGER. Manager is a lower-case label for Parts that influence or attempt to influence other Parts. Blockers are also managers.

MEMORY RECONSOLIDATION: The technical term for the process of reactivating a memory, neutralizing its emotional content, and permanently reconsolidating the change.

MISMATCH: Once the targeted emotional memory has been reactivated and become destabilized, the SIM Part embedded in the memory is confronted with a mismatch between what, based upon the content of the memory, it expects and what happens, such as a pleasant wind that carries away its pain. That mismatch neutralizes the emotional memory and leads to the final step of reconsolidation.

MONSTER. A Freestanding Part wearing the costume of a potentially scary creature. It can be a child Part wearing the costume to keep others at a distance or it can be dressed as a monster to carry out an errand for a powerful manager. When one interferes with the therapy, it's fairly easy to unmask the young Part inside with an unmasking intervention.

NEUTRALIZE: The primary means by which traumatic or other painful memories are healed. Following, the intervention, the originally painful or otherwise high energy experience becomes emotionally neutral.

PARTS: Also known as subpersonalities, ego states, voices, sides, and several dozen other names. They are the normal divisions of what most people think of as the indivisible self.

PARTS PSYCHOLOGY: The original name for Parts and Memory Therapy. Name of the book published in 2011.

PMDD: Premenstrual Dysphoric Disorder.

PMS: Premenstrual syndrome.

P&MT: Abbreviation for Parts and Memory Therapy.

SIM PART: Every memory has a Stuck in-the-Memory (SIM) Part embedded within it. There must be; otherwise, there would be no memory. This is the Part that directly experienced the event. Generally, such a SIM Part has only the one memory. However, when a second event occurs close in time or similarity to the first event, the same SIM Part may be found in both memories.

STEP-BACK TECHNIQUE: A temporizing procedure to help a patient create distance from a blending Part sharing an uncomfortable emotion or body sensation, such as crying, anger, or even a headache.

STUCK-IN-THE-MEMORY PART: See SIM Part.

SUD SCALE: The "Subjective Units of Disturbance (or Distress)" measures the patient's subjective sense of how disturbing or distressing a memory is at any given moment. The scale measures 11 levels of energy, from zero to 10.

SUE SCALE: The "Subjective Units of Energy" (SUD) scale measures the patient's—or a Part's--sense of how much energy is captured in a given memory at any given moment. There are 11 levels of energy from zero to 10. The scale measures positive energy or energy that is not negative. Useful when a patient cannot decide that a memory is a positive or negative one.

TWINNING: A calming or temporizing technique in which the patient temporarily places her fatigue, stress, or other negative emotions or body sensations into an imagined twin and then directs that twin in neutralizing its now current-time distress. It does not neutralize memories from the past, but it generally helps the patient to be calmer or more centered in the present.

UNMASKING: The process of removing the costume worn by a Part playing the role of a significant other, especially introjects and monsters. Typically, these entities require unmasking because they interfere with the therapy and cannot be convinced to work with the therapist and Conscious Self to achieve a better life.

INDEX

A

Abnormal, vii, 17, 57
Abreaction, 9
Abuse
    chronic, 111, 119,127, 135
    emotional, 74, 103
    memories of, 21, 93
    physical, 104
    sexual, 111
    significant, 21
Abuser, 35, 36, 102
Addiction, 152-154
    alcohol, 33. 152
    behavioral, 33
    drug, 33, 152
    gambling, 152
    pornography, 33, 118, 152
    shoplifting, 33,152
    smoking, 152
    treatment protocol, 152-154
Actor-child Part, 111
Affect bridge, 28, 52, 78, 97, 120, 143, 151, 154, 155, 160, 165
Age of Parts, 29, 58, 59-60, 73, 99
Age progression intervention, 111-114
Alcohol, 33, 152, 153
Alter personality, xiii, 18, 54, 57, 116
Amnesia, 18-22, 61
Anger, 3, 8, 9, 16, 20, 26, 27, 29, 30, 124, 129, 131-132
    manager, 20
Angry Part,2, 6, 27, 29, 30-32, 52-53, 58, 69, 82, 110, 120-121, 129.
Anxious, 5, 25, 30, 43, 85, 157, 158
Apology from abuser, 111
Apetite change, 157
Artifact, 70
Assagioli, R., viii, 163
Attachment loss, 153, 161
Attitude, 14, 15, 68, 124, 135

B

Belief, false, 82, 87, 109
Binging, 4
Blend(ed), 3, 5, 6, 27, 32, 40, 41, 54, 61, 63, 80, 126, 131, 134, 167, 169
Blob, 60, 67, 108, 109

Blocker, 81-84, 93, 98, 99-102, 109, 110, 117, 127, 130-138, 141-142, 145, 146 155 166, 167
Blocking
    by earlier memory, 50, 88, 96-99, 155
    by FS Part, See Blocker
Body sensation, 14, 15, 16, 25, 26, 28, 36, 44, 46, 78, 100, 120, 139, 140, 143, 145, 146, 159, 160, 169,
Breasts, tender or swollen, 157
Bloated, feeling, 157
Bridge, affect, See Affect bridge
Bulimic, 4
Butterflies, 25
Bystander Part, 41 80, 109

C

Coconscious Part, 3, 4, 61, 126
Cognitive behavioral therapy, 157
Concentrating, difficulty, 93, 94, 157
Confused, 21, 104, 158
Conscious Self, 5, 6, 7, 15, 24, 36, 39, 40, 44, 47, 51, 54, 56, 58, 61, 62, 63, 64, 78, 80, 87, 114115, 123, 126, 131, 132, 136, 144, 149, 165, 170
Consciousness, 3, 4, 7, 16, 17
Container
    for Two-Step technique, 82-84, 117, 126, 128, 142, 146
    for unprocessed SUD, 133-134
Cramping, 155, 158
Craving certain foods, 157, 158
Crying, 156, 158, 168

D

Death, 49, 147
Define the problem, 13, 15, 139, 144
Demon, 60, 99
Depressed, 15, 115, 133, 146, 157, 158
Destabilize emotional memory, 9-11
Devil, 3
Diagnosis vs Symptoms, 14
DID, 54, 61, 116
Dissociated memories, 16
Dissociation, viii, 16, 17, 18, 101, 135
Dissociation, normal, 11, 18, 101

172 INDEX

Dissociative identity disorder, 13, 18, 54, 57, 61, 116
Disturbance, subjective units of, 47, 117, 148, 168
Disturbing memory, 66, 70, 71, 77, 78, 88, 97, 102, 110, 131, 140, 143, 145, 151, 154, 155. 160
Divorce, 19, 20, 59
Dizzy/fainting, 158
Dream maker, 35-36
Duvarci, S. 8, 163
Dysfunction, 3, 8, 10, 123

E

Ego state, vii. ix, 1, 2, 9, 80, 88, 103, 165
Elicit the memories that are the foundation for the problem, 145, 13, 23, 75,
Emotion, not fact, disappears, 118
Emotion words,71, 146
Emotional memory, 8, 9, 11, 21, 55, 62, 63, 75, 76, 81, 83, 84, 88, 89, 105, 118, 127, 134, 138, 154, 162
Emotional state, 3
Ending a session with unfinished neutralizing, 133, 134-135
Ending therapy 109
Energy
    high-energy, 3, 6, 17, 39, 71, 76, 87, 147, 148, 168
    negative, 4, 36, 47, 50, 80, 82, 92, 101, 123, 124, 127, 128
    positive, 34, 46, 47
    SUD, 47, 48, 72, 92. 169
Excoriation, x, 150, 151
Executive control, 13, 18, 20, 61, 116
Extinction therapy, 102

F

Fatigue, 45, 46, 158, 169
Fear, 3, 8, 16, 36, 57, 65, 78, 81, 82, 83, 89, 90, 91, 94, 97, 128, 127, 135, 142, 146, 161
Fearful Part, 6
Fibromyalgia, x, 154-156
Find the Part that carries the problem, xi, 23, 67, 75, 137, 139
Fine, C., 5, 164
Fire, ball of, 3, 60, 68
Fire intervention, 72, 76, 83, 87, 90, 91, 95, 105, 114, 114, 122, 141, 145, 151. 155, 160
Forgetful, 18, 158
Freestanding Part, 2-5, 18, 24, 28-39, 54, 29, 126, 167, 168
Freudian, 2
FS Part, See Freestanding Part

G

Gerrish, W.G.,164
Grief, 8, 82

H

Hair-pulling, 150
Hallbreich, U.,157, 164
Headache,
High-energy, 3, 6, 17, 39, 71, 76, 87, 147, 148, 168
Hiller, W., 164
Hopeless, 157
Hotspot protocol, 147
Hurricane intervention, 91-92
Hypersomnia,157, 158
Hypnosis, 9, 57, 165
Hypnotherapy, 109, 111

I

IBS, x, 154, 155, 167
Implicit emotional memory, 8, 9, 76, 118, 163
Inner voice, 1, 2, 24, 86, 88, 112, 165, 169
Inscape, v, 25, 5, 44, 83, 102, 167
Insomnia, 157, 158
Intervention,
    return problem to source 123-124
    with fire, See Fire.
    with water, See Water.
    with wind,See Wind.
Internal family systems, viii, 10, 165
Interventions, blocked, 96-102.108-110, 132
Introject,
    complex example of, 110-111
    definitionof, 167
    father, 103, 117
    mother, 99, 103-107, 117, 124
    parent, 38-39, 93, 102-103,105-106, 142, 146, 167
    perpetrator, 43 99
    unmasking the, x, 85, 93, 105-109, 138, 168, 169
Irritable bowel syndrome, See IBS.

J

Jungian, 2

K

Keys, S.L.,164
Killing of a Part, 37, 132
Kleinstauber, M.,157, 164
Kluft, R.B., 57, 164

L

Lethargic, 157
Letting go of love, x, 148-149
    for an affair partner, 148-149

INDEX   173

for the good of the team, 148-149
for a long-lost love, 148-149
Lies by Parts, 58-59
Love,
   letting go of, x. 148-149
Lump in the throat, 25, 100
Lustyk, M.K.B., 157, 164

M
Maldonado, H., 8
Manager,
   definition, 167
   fear of disappearing, 142, 147
   fear of losing power, 97, 142
Marriage, 19, 59, 97
Memory
   autobiographical, 6, 10, 21, 28, 47, 53, 54, 67-70, 75, 76, 88, 118, 167
   dissociated, 16, 62
   earliest, 23, 24, 53, 70-72, 77, 88, 96-98, 110, 117, 119, 120, 140, 143, 145, 149, 151, 154
   emotional, See Emotional memory
   explicit, 89, 89
   as factual history, 88, 118
   hidden, 114-118
   implicit, See implicit emotion.
   indelible, 8, 50, 76
   reactivated, 80, 81, 149, 168
   reconsolidation, ii, 8-11, 50, 76, 84, 86, 102, 125, 148, 163, 165, 168
   scene, 32, 40, 41, 50, 79, 92, 95, 110, 117, 120, 123, 125, 130, 145, 155
   set, 3, 54, 64, 77-79, 82, 87, 113, 126, 143, 144
   themed, See Themed mories.
   wisdom from, 88, 90, 119, 123
Metaphor, 34, 85, 88, 92, 33, 146
Mind, viii, 2, 25, 26, 27, 55, 56, 58, 62, 69, 73, 88, 120, 138, 139, 143, 149, 153, 159
Mirror, 25, 135, 140, 153, 159
Mismatch, 10, 76, 84, 167
Molestation,. 35, 108
Monster, 3, 60, 68, 69, 102, 105, 108, 109, 168, 169
Mood state, 3

N
Nader, K., 8, 163
Nail-biting,
Naming,
Narrative
   autobiographical, 22, 50-51, 167

   eliciting, in neutralizing, 95, 147, 148
   factual, 118, 119
   hotspot, 147, 148, 162, 167
   recovery, 147, 148
Nausea, 155, 161
Negative emotions, returning them to their source, 123, 124
Nervous tension, 116, 158
Neural pathway, 10
Neurological, 8
Neuroscientific, 16, 158
Neuroscientists, 16, 158
Neutralize the problem memories, xi, 13, 23, 69, 75, 137, 141, 143, 145,
Neutralizing,
   blocking of, See Blocker, blocking.
   current time memories, 123
   current time stress, 44, 122
   distorted memories of introjects, 104, 105
   metaphors for, See Metaphor.
   resistance to, 100, 126-127, 129, 142, 146
   secret memories, 114-115
Nonconscious mind, 2, 55, 87
Noricks, J., ix, 9, 11, 47, 71, 76, 87, 165
Novel, 59

O
Obsessive-compulsive, 150
Onychophagia, 150
Out of control feeling, 31, 157
Overeating, 157
Overwhelm, 31, 45, 55, 57, 62, 64, 94, 122, 136, 138, 157, 158, 166

P
Pain, joint or muscle, 157
P&MT, v, vii, ix, 1, 2, 4, 13, 23, 39, 50, 54, 61, 67, 75, 76, 77, 87, 109, 111, 132, 137, 138, 142, 152-154, 159-160, 161, 168
Palpitations, 158
Panic attack, 35, 36, 43
Paranoid, 15
Part,
   actor-child, 111
   addicted, 33, 134-153, 154-155
   angry, See Angry Part.
   child, 6, 21, 28, 48, 53, 58, 65, 74, 99, 103, 104, 106, 107, 111-114, 118, 121, 168
   critical, 36-37
   definition of, 109
   Freestanding, 2, 3-5, 7, 18, 24, 36, 59, 74, 86, 115, 126
   FS, See Freestanding.

fuzzy type of, 5, 7-8
memory gatekeeper, 114, 115
not-me, 33, 34
punitive, 36-37, 84-85
romantic, 32, 35, 149-150
sexual, 32
SIM, See SIM Part.
skeptical, 32-33, 69, 85-86
Stuck-in-the-Memory, 2, 6-7, 39-41, 51, 87-88, 148, 160, 169
Stuck-in-time, 7
taskmaster, 32, 63, 64
teenage, 28, 32, 74, 117, 118
Pedreira, M.E., 8
Permission from blockers, 82, 92, 93, 96, 97, 100-101, 109, 117, 126, 130, 142, 146, 155, 156
Perpetrator introjects, 93
Personality, 2, 3, 5, 6, 19, 37, 103, 116, 131. 164
PMDD
    diagnosis, 156
    remission of, ii. 157. 159, 167,
    symptoms, 156, 158, 159-160
PMDD treatment protocol, 157, 159
PMS, symptoms. 156, 158, 159, 168
Pornography, 15, 33, 47, 70, 118, 152, 153, 154,
Postpartum depression, 147, 165
Premenstrual dysphoric disorder, 156
Premenstrual syndrome, 156, 164, 169
Protocol
    foundational, 13, 23, 67, 75, 137, 138, 139, 162,
    for addictions, x, 152, 153
    for excoriation, x, 150, 151
    for fibromyalgia, x, 155
    for hotspot trauma, x, 14, 147, 148, 162, 167
    for IBS, x, 154, 155
    for letting go of love, 148-149
    for nail-biting, 150-151
    for PMDD, x, 156, 157, 159, 160
    for premenstrual dysphoric disorder, 15
    for shortcut, x, 142, 144
    for training, x, 138-142
    for shy children, 138, 161-162
    for skin-picking, 150-151
    for trichotillomania, x, 150-151
Psychotherapy, v, vii, ix, 1, 5, 8, 9, 33, 76, 163, 164, 165
Puberty, 29, 111, 113
Purge, 4, 5
Purging, 4, 5

R
Rage, 31, 58, 131

Recenter, 43
Reconsolidation, 8-10, 50, 76, 77, 84, 86, 102, 148, 163, 164, 165, 168
Reframing, 53, 64
Reify, 57
Rejection sensitivity, 156
Rescue intervention, 95, 141, 145
Resistance to neutralizing, due to
    belief that emotional memory protects, 127, 128
    continuing abuse, 127
    fear of becoming weak, 128
    fear of loss of emotional guide, 129
Ritual, neutralizing, 34, 39, 89, 91, 101, 102, 106, 107, 108, 109, 122, 123, 124, 129, 130-131
Role, new, for Parts, 38, 132, 135, 136
Romantic love, 15, 47, 70, 82, 149-150

S
Sad Part, 6, 90, 91, 94
Sadness, 3, 10, 26, 82, 89, 90, 91, 94, 96, 124, 156, 159
Safe place, 94, 95, 141. 145, 167
Scared, 35
Schwartz, R.C., viii, ix, 9, 10, 76, 165
Secret memories, neutralizing, 114, 115
Self, viii, ix, 2, 3, 56, 14, 18, 43, 44, 47, 51, 54, 56, 57, 58, 61, 62, 63, 64, 65, 78, 80, 85, 86, 87, 94, 114, 115, 121, 123, 126, 127, 131, 132, 136, 144, 152, 168, 170
Self-esteem, 1, 165, 14, 139, 144
Self-states, 1, 165
Serotonin reuptake inhibitor, 157, 164
Set, memory, 54, 55, 64, 77-78, 81, 82, 87, 113, 126, 143, 144
    unique, 3, 85
Sex abuse, 35
Shaver, S., 164
Shoplifting addiction, 33, 152
Shortcut protocol, x, 142, 144
Sides, viii, 1, 88, 169
Significant memory, 7, 39, 47, 52, 72, 77, 149, 156
Silent abreaction, 9, 76, 165, 166
SIM Part as target, 48, 50, 55, 77, 82-83, 86, 87, 88, 92, 94, 95, 96, 101, 115, 116, 123, 124, 125, 140, 141, 144, 145, 146, 149, 155, 160, 168, 169
SIM Parts in the third person, 40, 41, 65, 79, 80, 81, 125-126, 140, 141, 151, 160
Skin-picking, 150, 151
Somatic bridge, 143, 145
Step away technique, 41

Step back technique, x, 26, 33, 44, 62, 64, 169
Step forward, 26
Stress relief, Twinning technique for, 45, 122
Stuck in time, 7
Stuck-in-the-Memory, See SIM
Subjective units of disturbance, See SUD scale
Subjective units of energy, See SUE scale
Subpersonality, 1, 2, 88, 97
SUD scale, 47, 48, 49-54, 59, 62-65, 77, 87, 88, 91-97, 98, 101-102, 117, 118, 124-129, 131, 141-142, 146-160, 169
SUE scale, 47-49, 51-54, 72, 92, 149, 169
Surgery, open-heart, 118
Surrogate, x, 103, 138, 161, 162
Suspicious, 158
Swollen hands or feet, 158
Symbolic, 3, 9, 10, 60, 83, 141, 145, 151, 155, 160
Symbolism, 60
Synaptic, 9

T

Talk therapy, 102
Taskmaster, 32, 63, 64
Temporizing, 43, 138, 169, 170
Tense, 14, 157
Theme, 7, 29, 32, 39, 55, 70
Themed memories, 3, 29, 55, 74, 75, 143, 144
Therapy helper, 64
Third-person point of view, 41, 79, 121, 125, 126, 140, 141, 145, 160
Ticic, R., 163, 164
Tightness in the chest, 25, 44, 100
Trauma,
　general, viii, ix, x, 17, 57, 62, 64, 76, 94, 95, 102, 109, 119, 123, 124, 127, 143, 147, 148, 153, 164, 165, 167
　as murder, witness, 84, 94
　as rape, 63, 94, 108, 109
　sexual, 108, 111
　as torture, 63, 94
Trauma-like, ix, 8, 45, 153, 167
Trauma scene, 76, 94, 95, 141, 145
Traumatic, 6, 8, 9, 18, 40, 62, 63, 64, 76, 95, 133, 143, 147, 148, 164, 169
Trichotillomania, x, 150-151
Trigger, 7, 9, 27, 45, 49, 62, 96
Troubling, 9, 72, 143
Twin, 46, 170

Twinning intervention, x, 43, 44, 45-46, 138, 170
Two-fishermen-with-a-net-intervention, 27, 28, 140, 153, 159
Two-Step intervention, 82, 84, 98, 101, 109, 117, 126, 128, 142, 146

U

Unblocking, 81-86
Unburdening, ix, 9, 10, 76
Uncomfortable symptom, 51, 58, 169
Unmasking,
　introject, x, 85, 93, 102, 105, 106, 107, 138, 168, 170
　hidden child Part, 106
　monster, 105, 108, 109, 168, 170
　ritual, 106-108, 109
Usual activities, lost interest, 157, 158

V

Vacation, going on,
　by a Part between sessions, 134
　by a Part at the end of therapy, 38, 133, 135
　by an addicted Part, 135
Visualization, 8, 9, 10, 109, 141, 145
Visualize, 3, 10, 11, 14, 15, 28, 35, 37, 46, 64, 65, 81, 89, 90, 92, 95, 100, 116, 122, 123, 124, 132, 134, 141, 153, 160, 167
Voice, See Inner voice.

W

Walker, M., 8
Waterfall intervention, 46, 80, 89, 115, 116, 117, 162
Watkins, H.H., viii, ix, 9, 76, 165, 166
Watkins, J., viii, ix, 9, 78, 143, 165, 166
Wind intervention, 72, 76, 80, 81, 83, 89, 90-92, 95, 96, 101, 115, 123, 130, 141, 142, 145, 146, 155, 160, 168
Witthoft, M., 164
Work-around, 78, 115, 161
World views, 69

www.ingramcontent.com/pod-product-compliance
Lightning Source LLC
Chambersburg PA
CBHW031314150426
43191CB00005B/221